Headlong into Pennilessness

Published by ACM Retro Ltd,
The Grange,
Church Street,
Dronfield,
Sheffield S18 1QB.

Visit ACM Retro at:
www.acmretro.com

A catalogue record for this book is available from the British Library.

Cover shot: A boy is solemnly christened: (left to right) Harold, Dorothy, Mabel, Pat, Ken, Auntie Harriet.

Foreword

Foreword

As poet, art critic and occasional fabulist, I have written hundreds of thousands of words in my life. But I have not written this book about my early life in Sheffield. Until now. When I think about that fact, it strikes me as both odd and inevitable. This, surely, is the book that has been sitting patiently on my back doorstep all my adult life, asking to be written. But, for a variety of reasons, it has not been written. Why though? As a writer for newspapers, I have always felt that my responsibility was towards the present and to that-which-was-just-about-to-come-into-being. It is difficult to make sense of the present. There is always so much of it. It never stops coming. One does one's best, which is seldom quite enough. The past, however, is a different country altogether. It feels remote, fragmentary, insufficient. After all, we were never there, were we? It is the stuff of historians and learned antiquarians. We smaller creatures, on the other hand, forever rooted in the present, cannot seem to stop ourselves surging, pell mell, into the future, helplessly in the grip of its promises. It is the present and the future which seem to need our attention. Why demand of oneself more than that? And then there is the issue of nostalgia, that fabrication of pasts which may not quite have happened. Is not nostalgia a kind of sickness, a yearning, above all things else, to falsify?

The demand to look backwards came about quite serendipitously. My publisher, Neil Anderson, asked me a little over a year ago whether I had written any poems about my home town of Sheffield, where I had lived continuously for the first nineteen years of my life. He was preparing a *Sheffield Miscellany* for publication. Yes, a few, I discovered, though not too many. Quickened by his interest, that rather sorry few eventually became many more than just a few, and that journey back to those poems, and to the experiences that they had striven to encapsulate, led me to reflect upon my own past in ways that had never quite happened before. Those fragmentary, insufficient memories provoked other memories. The loose, the wayward, the insubstantial grew into something more definite and meaningful. All those errant snatchings became captive within the pages of a book. This book. I had discovered that the harder you push against the door of the past, the further it opens.

And yet even as I turn my face back from the present, I recognise a certain fearfulness. It is so easy to misrepresent what has gone before, so easy to tell politically convenient lies. It is also exhausting to confront everything that you were, to recognise the mistakes, the petty, brazen acts of wilful subterfuge, the paths not taken. The past can rob you of the strength and confidence to face forward into the future. And yet there it all seemingly is, so complete unto itself in its own way, shimmering in a falsifyingly beguiling mist of sorts. The past is ever ready to beckon and to ensnare you. There is a comfort in cozying up to it. The past itself will tell you that if you choose to invite its opinion. As you creep back in its direction, you find yourself inhabiting past selves.

As I was bent slightly forward writing these words on my iPad, in a farmhouse in the South of France which overlooked fields of freshly opened sunflowers - I knew that I needed to get as far away as possible from my origins in order to gain access to what I would be struggling to re-discover about myself - my wife showed me a photograph that she had just taken of me on her Iphone, bent of back, hunched forward at my task.

I looked exactly like my late mother, Dorothy, at her kitchen table in Totley, where she spent the last thirty years of her life, purple woollen shawl thrown across her shoulders - she was always starving, as she put it, even on the warmest of days - counting the change from her pension, apportioning it to one or another of the many small, see-through envelopes that were so eagerly waiting to receive it. There were always so many of those envelopes.

A big sister's helping hand:
Pat and Michael beside the rockery in the
back yard at 45 Coningsby Road, c. 1958

Back Yard Scene, Fir Vale, Sheffield, 1957

Who is this fresh-faced little whippersnapper at the back door, grinning from ear to ear for all he's worth, sitting on that tired, wonky red pouffe he's been struggling to carry out of the kitchen in his pale, stick-thin arms? His arms are crossed as if he really belongs there in his own backyard, with his bare feet on hot hot asphalt, in front of the partly open kitchen window – phew, it wasn't half hot, that summer's day in 1957! – and with an empty milk bottle balanced on the window sill just behind his head.

There are usually two of those bottles sitting there, waiting patiently to be collected by the milk man, once up to the brim with full-cream milk. The best bit is when you peel off the silver lid, and dip your finger into the top for a quick fingerful of clarty yellow cream, and then try to stick the lid back on again, straight and smooth. Some hopes. He's partial to a glass or two of milk. Especially at bedtime. A few years, on when he'll be taking the bus down through Page Hall from Firth Park Grammar School, he'll see an advertising hoarding from the top deck with that famous slogan he'll never be able to get out of his head: drinka pinta milka day... When the empties are put out, late at night, for the milk man to chink together as he collects them between his two fingers early in the morning – he usually comes right early, in the dark in winter, before anyone's up and about – there'll be a couple of yellow plastic milk tokens neatly piled up next to them, as if they're counting themselves just to check. He quite likes those milk tokens, the rough feel of what's written on them. They look a bit like light, yellow, plastic money.

He loves it in this back yard in north-east Sheffield, you can tell that by the way he's smiling, can't you? Summer will never end. The back door, half open as you can see, will never quite close. His grandmother Mabel has already been across the yard to the outside lavvy to empty out the pongy chamber pot that lives underneath the bed in the front bedroom. Soon his mother will come out to hang up his sister's daft blue school knickers on the line for him to laugh at and poke sticks at. His tousled, curly hair needs a bit of a cut by Alf the barber on Fir Vale Bottom in the back room of Mr Hobson the Hairdresser's, but he doesn't really mind that because while he's sitting there, dangling his legs, waiting for his turn, he'll be reading The Broons and Oor Wullie in the Scottish comics they always have at the barber's shop. Goodness knows why. He loves it that they're there though, all stacked up in an untidy heap. He loves Oor Wullie best of all, that little, mischievous, ginger-haired lad who sits outside his own back door in Scotland on an upturned bucket in his blue dungarees. That's why he's sitting like he is just now, because he wants to look a bit like Oor Wullie. He wants to be ready for anything. And he is.

It's a funny place, that barber's. The front room facing the street is especially set aside for women sitting under great big hairdryers - they look like shiny helmets. Mr Hobson himself works in that bit, all dressed up in his fancy blue shortie tunic with scissors sticking out of the top pocket. He doesn't half fuss over women's hair. He's a funny bloke, Mr Hobson, always dashing about so much. Funny hair an' all - all crinkly waves and the stink of brilliantine. The only bit about going to the barber's the lad doesn't like is the last part, when Alf pours out some of that thick, green, smeary stuff from a bottle into the centre of his palms, slathers and squeezes it around a bit - you can see him doing it in the big mirror - and then rubs it like billyo into his hair before combing it flat in two directions, one bit to the left of the parting, the other to the right. He doesn't like flat hair, and partings are boring. He can't wait to get it all messed up and springy again like it is now. He can't wait for it to be all going straight back again like papa's does.

Nothing will ever change, will it? That's not really true though. So much has changed already, though this house hasn't seen much of it. That doorstep has been lovingly dubbined white like this by some woman in her house slippers, scrattin' on her bony knees, trying not to ladder her precious nylons, for as long as anyone can remember, and nobody would want it any other way because this is a respectable family with high standards. Other things have gone though – not that this little lad would know anything about most of it. Kids just live in the present, don't they? So we'll just have to tell him. When he's not smiling into his mother Dorothy's Brownie camera with its smart brown canvas cover that you snap shut with a press

11

stud – that's why he's smiling so much, because his mother's smiling back at him from behind that little camera - he's probably looking directly across from him at the green wooden shed next to the outside lavatories where grandfather Harold keeps his big motorbike, that blinking BSA. That shed's been there forever. Except that it hasn't. Not long before he was born – that must have been about eight years ago - there was an Anderson shelter where it now stands, built by Harold, to keep the family and the next door neighbours safe from the Germans bombers, which blitzed Sheffield two nights in a row eight years before he was born. He wasn't even alive when that happened, and if you're not alive, how can you possibly know something feelingly – I mean really know?

So that's gone - as are the ration books that people still had to use, even after the war was over. In fact, this little lad will see so much disappear during his lifetime. Fine Victorian buildings in the centre of town which the Germans accidentally spared will be destroyed by civic vandalism. After the Second World War, the city council created a lovely garden beside the town hall called The Peace Gardens where, when he becomes an angry, confused teenager, he will sit, on a wooden bench with the Victorian Town Hall at his back, and read a tortured autobiographical novel called *Querelle of Brest* by a Frenchman called Jean Genet. That garden will be demolished in due course for no good reason at all, and it will be replaced by a harsh and ugly square straight out of the pattern books of Fascist Italy.

The steel industry, that mighty employer, once the pride of Sheffield, will also disappear in a puff of smoke. The Don Valley, where the Bessemer furnaces were still pouring out their giant cups of molten metal when this boy was sitting on his wonky pouffe in the sunshine, will vanish. In their place will spring up a huge, purpose-built arena for rock concerts, an outpost of Mercedes-Benz, the German car maker, and other delights of the future. Yes, the Germans will have returned, but this time we will smile at them, and shake their hands in friendship, and buy their beautiful cars. That is this boy's future. I know that for a fact because this boy sitting in the sun on his bucket was me.

Fir Vale

I grew up at 45 Coningsby Road, Fir Vale, Sheffield 5. A single number was quite enough of a postal code in those days. Ah, Fir Vale! I often used to think about those two words, fir and vale, when I walked the streets of my neighbourhood as a child and young man. They seemed bizarrely inappropriate. They conjured up a tranquil rural spot, fit for an English poet perhaps, a place set apart from the hubbub of the world. Fir Vale was indeed at the bottom of a valley, but there was precious little hint of the rural or the tranquil about it in the 1950s. The tram would descend the hill down Barnsley Road to a crossroads and a set of traffic lights. At or near that busy intersection there were shops – the greengrocer's beside the tram stop back into town; Banners the haberdashery where my mother's loose change from buying biased binding used to arrive, whisked through the air along a length of wire, in a little metal canister; Gabbitas' the newsagent and sweetshop; the Fir Vale Post Office; Olive Fields, the posh hairdresser's for all those women who wanted permed blue hair; two churches, an Anglican Church for the well-to-do and a Methodist Church, with its mighty steeple that could be seen for miles around, for the slightly less so; a huge, old cinema called the Sunbeam; the chemist, with its big weighing machine for stepping on, where my mother always bought her glass bottles of cod liver oil and malt, which she would later administer to me by spoonsful so nasty and so thick that they nearly made you sick when you tried to swallow them; Mr Brown the toyshop down towards Owler Lane whose tall, narrow front window always seemed to be full of Matchbox and Dinky Toys sitting on top of their tiny yellow boxes - fire engines, saloon cars and even sleek red racing cars you could rock back and forth in the palm of your hand - that you could never stop yourself wanting to buy; and grandest of all, the double-gated entrance to what is now the Northern General Hospital, a sprawling site which included forbidding Victorian buildings that had once housed a workhouse and, in my childhood, a tramps' ward. No tranquillity there then. And certainly very few hints of the rural.

It is difficult to conjure the atmosphere of those post-war decades in Fir Vale. There was such drabness, greyness then. There were no bathrooms in our street in Fir Vale, no washing machines, no showers, no refrigerators. Stuff that needed to be kept cold – butter, milk, meat – was stored on high, rickety shelves (mice didn't climb that far) in the pantry, which was nothing but the space at the top of a set of chilly, unsmooth stone steps that led down from the kitchen to the cellar, where my grandmother did her cheese-making, stringing it up in little, saggy, smelly bags of muslin that dripped

13

milky-looking watery stuff. People sparkled less in every way. They looked deeply unattractive. Clothes seemed old and drab. People smelled. Hair went unwashed for days on end. No one flaunted his or her own sexiness. No one walked along the Bottom at Fir Vale flirtatiously or coquettishly. There was no sexiness. What would have been the point of it? Sex was simply not on the agenda for so many people. As Philip Larkin once remarked, making a vague stab in the right direction, sex was not invented until 1963. The unclothed bodies of Fir Vale did not hold the promise of a fragrant allure. No one was yearning to peel off those clothes in order to savour sweet-smelling, sweet-looking human flesh. Old, unfashionable, not-so-clean clothes of the kind most often worn in Fir Vale were best removed in the dark, and very quickly too, because bedrooms were always s-so b-bloody c-cold. And anyway, who would ever have wanted to go to bed with one of our fierce and argumentative neighbours, that woman with big, beefy arms and her hair stuck in curlers underneath a head scarf, for example, until the minute before she hard-slammed the front door, gostering away, for Saturday night down at the Cannon Hall where she'd be able to let her hair down for an hour or two?

What is more, serious disease was much more rife then than it is now. You saw a lot of polio victims everywhere, sad children with their legs in irons, men with clubbed feet walking along as briskly as they could, trying to put a brave face on their afflictions. The blue and pink plaster polio boy, arm stuck straight out, with the beckoning palm and honey-coloured hair, so pale and so frightening, used to stand outside the chemist's on Page Hall, waiting for a donation so that he'd be able to help children like himself not catch it in the future. It was so often, in those straitened times, a matter of getting through life, with a modicum of dignity. And yet Fir Vale did harbour nooks and crannies of what can only be described as rural promise.

When the Queen graciously deigned to pay a post-coronation visit in 1954 - we waited for her with flags in Herries Road; we even caught a fleeting glimpse of her motorcade, the big, posh, black Daimler she was travelling in, as serious and slow-moving as a hearse - she was said to have noticed and remarked upon a row of lovely thatched cottages at the bottom of Barnsley Road, just before you reached the traffic lights. I remember those thatched cottages, set inside their low, drystone walls, amidst lusciously combed green grass. They were a wonderful sight, so bizarre, so anachronistic, so... yes, rural. The rural displaced to the city. Or a remnant of the rural left and lost in the ever encroaching city. I also remember stepping inside one of these cottages once, and of talking to the mother of the unattractive girl who lived there. What I remember most of the visit on that fine afternoon was the terrible smell of damp as I stood in the hall. It positively reeked of it underneath that thatched hat of a roof. My mother later told me in no uncertain terms that old cottages were very unhealthy places to be living. By the 1960s those cottages had been demolished. When she made this reference to a house whose living quarters were protected by nothing more substantial than a poor, straw roof, my mother was probably thinking back, albeit glancingly, to her own childhood at Crimicar Lane, where she had lived with her mother, father and two younger brothers as a child and a young woman. That isolated, gimcrack sort of a house in a field, on the wild southern edge of Sheffield, had been made of brick - and wood. At least the home that I knew at Coningsby Road was built of something more solid, dependable and rain-proof: mortar and red bricks.

Crimicar Lane

My mother, Dorothy Alice Gladys Glover - I'm giving her the name you will find on her birth certificate in order to make her wince a little - had been unhappy at Crimicar Lane, in that little part-brick and part-wooden house with its nearby cricket pavilion owned by the YMCA. After returning from the First World War, my grandfather Harold had worked as a groundsman there, levelling the cricket pitch with the help of an enormous, horse-drawn, cast-iron roller that would have killed any child who happened to stray into its path. It wasn't much of a job working for a pittance as a groundsman, but at least it was regular work, and so much better than the first job he had managed to find after he got back from the war, which was repairing or building roads up Redmires way, that bleak, god-awful spot. What a way to treat a war hero! Amongst the good things about Crimicar Lane was a horse called Tommy, lovingly remembered by my mother Dorothy and her two younger brothers – my Uncles Ken and Norman – for its characterful idleness. Tommy would sit back on his rump when he had done enough just like an out-of-puff old lady trying to get her second wind. It was always never more than just enough for Tommy. One day, my grandfather Harold drove Tommy into the city to collect a consignment of coke for the boiler. Tommy paused for a well-earned rest in the city centre. The coke shot out of the back of the cart, all of it. God knows how many hours it took to scrape it all off the street.

Tommy came into his own on a Sunday. That was the day Harold would buff up his horse's harnesses until they gleamed, and take the family out for a stately progress in the horse and cart - never more rapid than stately - through the back roads of Derbyshire, to such places as Hathersage and Bakewell. Even the benediction of intermittent sunlight was reported on days such as those.

There were cricket teas on a Saturday, but little else by way of a social life on that unruly outer edge of the city – except of the kind that Dorothy herself invented. Dressing up her brothers for amateur dramatics, for example. There are photographs of Dorothy and her two brothers in the field outside the house. She looks as if she cares nothing about herself. Her face seems to suggests that her principal task in life is to oversee the enjoyments of Kenneth and Norman, her younger brothers. Her hair looks lank, unkempt, unwashed, and she is squinting through the frames of an ugly pair of spectacles. What boy would ever look at her? Chance would be a fine thing. Those younger brothers, by contrast, look boisterous, full of boyish venturesomeness, eager to be at play. An orphanage stood nearby, inhabited by poor children. My mother was afraid of them. They seemed so threatening in their old, hand-me-down, darned clothes. They had such lost looks. My mother was stuck somewhere in the middle. She was neither lost nor gainfully employed. She spent quite a lot of her later life mending clothes for other people. That was long before people got into the habit of throwing out newish clothes out of sheer boredom. The unimaginable luxuries of times to come!

She took piano lessons, fiercely supervised by my grandfather Harold. When she felt disinclined to practise, he would lock her into the room with the upright piano until she had served her allotted time at the keyboard. When the family moved down to Coningsby Road, to live in the house occupied by my grandmother's mother, Dorothy's spirits leaped. There would be shops, a cinema with its Hollywood idols twice a week, and other delights to savour. Her life would begin again. A few years later she met Sidney Glover, the father I never knew as a child.

Coningsby Road

At 45 Coningsby Road, that tiny, two-up, two-down, late-nineteenth-century terraced house (then owned by John Smith the local brewer) in north-east Sheffield, where I was born in 1949, and lived until I left home for university in the autumn of 1968 at the age of nineteen, life was always lived between here and there. There was the warmth of the kitchen, cramped, over-full with warring people and things - mother, uncle, sister, grandfather (we called him papa, with an accent on the first 'a'), nanny (our family name for a grandmother), and a black range with a blazing fire, which roared into life after papa had set it going with paper spills - made from screwed up lengths of the *Sheffield Star* - soon after dawn, and then religiously sustained it with buckets of coal from the cellar. And then, just a few steps across the asphalted back yard, there was the desolation of the outside lavatory with its indomitable red wooden door.

There was no alternative to that freezing, cupboard-like space, where the wind came shrieking under the door, and the rain quickly made a mockery of any pair of well polished black school shoes - the door stopped short about three inches above the cold concrete floor. Not a single house on that street had a bathroom or an inside lavatory. Nor would they ever have in those years. (This was one of the reasons why the local council came to regard them as fit only for demolition. No one had heard of bijou residences in those dark days). Worst of all were the visits to that monkish space on wet winter nights. It would always demand your attention in the end. You could only hold on for so long. Departure was often heralded by this turn of phrase: I'm just going across the yard. Occasionally someone would ask, mildly interested in the outcome: number one or number two? You never thought about the answer for too long. You never much bothered about smells in the outside lavvy either because there would always be blasts of driving wind to get rid of them in no time at all. No one ever lingered with his trousers down in that place.

Not everybody was sentenced life-long to go across to the lavvy. Some were granted exemption in the end. When my grandmother Mabel became too old to go across the back yard unaided, she urinated, long and splashily, legs wide spread, dress hitched to knee height, over a resonating bucket in the corner of the kitchen beside the back door - the very same place, as it happens, where, some years later, her husband (my grandfather Harold) chose to do his physical jerks in old age, often dressed only in his off-white long johns. He never missed a night. It wasn't half a sight for sore eyes, believe you me.

And yet, once inside there, that outside lavatory had its own strange appeal. It was a fine and private place - and even a bit of a makeshift reading room of sorts. There was the *Radio Times*, for example, torn into small squares, and skewered onto a re-modelled coat hangar, attached to the back of the wooden door, that served as lavatory paper before the era of the silky, bottom-pampering shop-bought stuff. I used to tear these ragged sheets off, one by one, and, pausing, read them. Dr Who was in its infancy in those years. I would read and re-read the summaries of the plot of last week's episode, turning over its excitements in my mind. The *Radio Times* was a harsh diet though. And on the eyes too in that gloomy spot. The comparative gentleness of shop-bought lavatory paper was a revelation some years into the future. I never once thought about what might happen to the newsprint. A small supermarket made its first appearance at Page Hall - just a short walk away from Fir Vale - at the beginning of the 1960s, when I was about eleven years old. We marvelled at the fact that there was so much to be bought, and all in the same shop, all those heaped up tins of mandarin oranges and Carnation Milk! Scrummy yummy!

Not everyone re-used their back issues of the *Radio Times*. Our next-door neighbour, Dennis Swift, would take entire scrolls of newspapers across the yard with him, tucked into his armpit. He was evidently digging in for the long haul. He might have been an Egyptologist if he'd been given half a chance. One day, towards the middle of the 1960s, Dennis Swift accidentally introduced me to one of my heroes. Until then lanky Dennis in glasses, likeable enough, had been nothing but a neighbour. Then I suddenly discovered that he was a close friend of Freddy Garrity of Freddie and the Dreamers, a pop group which rocketed to fame, albeit momentarily, when the Mersey Sound took the world by storm in 1963. Not that Freddy Garrity himself was a Liverboy. Like the rest of his band, he grew up in Manchester, and before becoming a pop star, he had been a milkman. By the time that Freddy arrived in our back yard, I knew very well what he looked like – he was a skinny, spidery man, smallish, with horn-rimmed spectacles and raggedy curls – and so when his white Rolls Royce eased itself up onto the pavement near our front window, I recognised that a very special kind of celebrity had arrived in Coningsby Road. I even saw him walking across our back yard to the outside lavatory, stepping jauntily, almost skippingly, as he was wont to do on *Ready, Steady, Go* when he sang 'How Do You Do What You Do To Me, I Wish I Knew...' He was not carrying a scroll of rolled up newspapers underneath his arm either. With the benefit of hindsight, I can now see that there was something pleasingly harmless about Freddie and his stage act. Although he somewhat resembled Buddy Holly, he lacked...true grit? When he danced in formation with his band on *Blue Peter* singing 'You were made for me' (that last word memorably pronounced may-ee), all four of them kicking their legs back like a line-up of jerky marionettes, he felt like pop's softest option. The lyrics seemed to confirm it:

You were made for me,
Everybody tells me so,
You were made for me,
Don't pretend that you don't know...'

Aside from the function for which it had been established, the outside lavvy had another use, and this was one that I prized highly. My mother and my maternal grandmother were extraordinarily incompetent cooks of green vegetables. Brussels sprouts, wrapped in pages of the local newspaper, quite robust, attractive and completely odourless when they first appeared from the greengrocer's which was situated beside the tram stop into town on Fir Vale Bottom, were very slowly reduced to slimy, slippery, mushy balls of a preternaturally eerie greenness as they were boiled and boiled in four inches of water in the aluminium saucepan on our kitchen stove. When I used to put one, gingerly, fearfully, into my mouth, the sour taste-cum-reek of it, hitting mouth and nostrils full force simultaneously, made me feel physically sick. They are still the most disgusting things I have ever tasted, and I've been around a bit by now.

Then, one day I hit on an ingenious solution. First of all I would press my tongue flat up against the roof of my mouth in order to eradicate the ability to taste anything whatsoever - that in itself struck me as a marvel. Having done that, I would then cram into my mouth as much sprout mush as it could contain, and, cheeks swollen like a hamster's, make a quick dash across the yard, rain or shine. I would then spit the whole lot into the lavatory bowl, and quickly pull the chain. An almighty rush of water, and it was all gone.

That lavatory, one of a connected pair, stood directly opposite the door of the green wooden shed where my grandfather kept his motorbike, and I stored my bicycle and a wooden hutch of assorted mice. Those white mice had eyes as red as reflector lights shining in the night. I loved mice, then and now. They were always so fast and so slippery.

All this was in the backyard, which opened out directly from our kitchen door. This yard was shared communally by four families, which meant that the back doors of four separate houses opened out into it. The biblical injunction to love one's neighbours had never seemed to be of more pressing relevance. Those four back doors included the one which belonged to the house at the very top of the yard, which, at the front, could be seen to be the very last house at that end of our street. That house was both a home and a shop-cum-beeroff. Yes, John Smith, one of the many local brewers, owned our houses when I was young. The local council acquired them later, which transformed these dwellings, abracadabra-like, into council houses. We became council tenants, with the attendant burden of social disapproval that belonging to such a community often seems to invite. We didn't feel any different though.

That backyard, a rectangular stretch of uneven asphalt inhabited by a shed, four knocked-about metal dust bins with bendy black rubber lids, the forbidding walls of a superannuated air raid shelter, four outside lavatories, and a rockery at the back of which a laburnum tree struggled to survive, was, in the eyes of many visitors, an unprepossessing space. I never found it so. I remember it with warmth and affection. I feel even now, as I contemplate its slight bleakness in my mind's eye, enveloped by its atmosphere, as if it is still warming and protecting me from a distance of more than fifty years. It had no garden to speak of. The rockery was always morbidly inhospitable to all species of plant life. My mother, who always loved the sight of flowers growing, had to content herself with a couple of flower pots on the window sill beside the milk bottles.

At the top end of the yard there was a forbidding-looking air raid shelter – more blockhouse, I always thought, than air raid shelter. It was a solid, square, brick structure, part underground and part above ground. I used to belt footballs against it to cut it down to size a bit, show it what's what, grunting out loud when the ball smashed against the wall. From our end of the yard I could see a deep-set, closed-off, window-like recess in the wall of the air raid shelter which faced us, quite close to the ground. Mysterious. Like someone who never speaks, I always thought. To gain entry to that building, you had to go up to the top of the yard and squeeze your way through into the bit of backyard owned by the beeroff, where stained brown wooden crates, and empty bottles reeking of stale beer, were often stacked higgledy-piggledy.

That shelter had a hugely heavy door. To reach it, you had to descend four cold stone steps – it always felt chilly, that place, even in the middle of summer, and a bit forbidding, even frightening – until you were half underground. The door of the shelter was made from solid, rusting metal which left a weird brown stain on your hands of the kind you should never lick, and it required a tremendous effort to push it back. Once inside, you groped your way towards a damp, dark inner chamber. The darkness inside there always felt so heavy - like a stack of house bricks bearing down on your head. It was also an ideal spot for telling ghost stories and imagining the worst that could possibly happen. An older, outsize boy in old, smelly clothes called Terry used to come around to do just that. We feared, and were a little thrilled, by the possibility of Terry's arrival, which was always unannounced. Terry who? you may well be asking yourselves. And from where? Not far, I knew that much. He was only ever Terry to us though, and he always came shuffling into the back yard, breathing quite hard. Perhaps he was asthmatic. That thought has only just occurred to me. Almost everything came unannounced in those days before telephones. And no one had a telephone at Coningsby Road. The world always took you by surprise - or announced its arrival from a great distance, usually by letter. My mother had her first telephone put in some time after the celebration of her sixty-fifth birthday. She was living the life of a newly re-married woman by then, and a telephone was part and parcel of her faster later life in posh Totley with Wilfred Welsby, a man in a trilby hat from Liverpool who, amongst many other assorted talents, knew his way around the underside of car bonnets.

At the back of the yard which faced our kitchen window, just behind an enormously high wall – I never quite understood why that wall needed to be quite so high, but I was mightily impressed by its height all the same - there was a small factory which made ventilation shafts. The silence of our back yard was often torn to shreds by the shrieking whine of oxy-acetylene torches from over that factory wall. When I walked up Herries Road in the general direction - God forbid - of Sheffield Wednesday's football ground, past the wonky, ill-fitting metal side gates to that factory - they got dragged shut at nights by a length of chain and a hefty padlock - I would often see short, sweating, greasy-handed men in blue overalls, wearing visors, bent over tall scrolls of metal, wielding spurting torches of intermittent flame. For a child of any age, there is always a modicum of excitement to be garnered from the sight of fierce flames on the loose.

Even though I have no doubts whatsoever that it rained in Sheffield just as much as it rained anywhere else, I still remember that back yard as characteristically sun-lit. I associate it with summer days beyond the reach of the dreary, standing-in-line-with-your-mouth-closed discipline and shut-awayness of school. I can still see myself sitting beside one of the grates in the centre of the yard into which rain water drained, the one which our kitchen window overlooked, from where I would often notice my mother, hands delving deep into sudsy washing-up water, smiling out at me as I sat there, legs splayed out to the side, playing with marbles, watching them turning and turning in ever diminishing circles. She looked like a picture in a frame. Or, on a slightly different summer's day, I would be sitting beneath that window once again, struggling to transform the rickety, temperamentally unstable wooden clothes horse into two walls with a pitched roof, and then throwing heavy blankets over it to make a dark and stifling tent of sorts in which to squat and scheme. Carol, our next-door neighbour until she took her hook with her parents to Canada, squeezed up against me once inside that tent and invited me to examine holes and what might go in them. I left, confused, pleading a sudden thirst for a glass of milk.

Fire Work Night

I loved that back yard. I could have lived in it. Some great things went off there. Fire Work Night, to name but one. It were great in them days, Fire Work Night. Every backyard on Coningsby Road had its own bonfire. There weren't half a commotion up and down our street, folks in hats and gloves, even owd folks, loitering at their own back doors, rubbing their hands and gesturing for all they were worth. Our Guy Fawkes man weren't up to much though. It never were. Nobody bothered enough. It were made from bits of Mum's old clothes and cast off bits of sheets - stuff you couldn't swap for pegs wi' t gypsies that came trundling along the street in their carts dragged by a sorry old nag - stuffed with straw, and then trundled down Herries Road in Pat's old doll's pram, and stuck outside Mr Latham's sweetshop on the Bottom. Mr Latham had a gammy leg - he jigged up and down as he walked towards you in his built up black boot - and he allus wore an old brown shop coat wi greasy pockets. He allus kept one hand stuck in his pocket an all, jingling coins as he went. He were forever jingling coins. He gave me my first job, two hours every Sat'day morning, ten sharpish to round about twelve, jumping up and down on old cardboard boxes that needed breaking up and flattenin into heaps in the yard at the back of the shop. Five shillings. Not bad. It were allus rainin' in that yard, right high brick walls an' all so you couldn't see out, and that cardboard were allus wet an slippery-slidey to jump on. I did it though. I never once broke my leg either.

We used to stand there on the pavement outside Mr Latham's sweetshop, holding this cast-off old cap of papa's, with that Guy Fawkes' daft head, wi' two buttons sewn on for eyes, half falling out of the pram, saying 'Penny for the guy, mester, please', and ones who weren't too full of themselves to stop and look - even for a second - after they 'd jumped off the tram to Lane Top, used to come up and laugh at us an' pat us on the head, or twist our ears as if we were a jug on t'table, and chuck us a penny, and poke at its eyes and say daft stuff like: is it real then, laddo? Oh ay, I used to say, oh ay, mester. Ask it summat. Owt. It allus answers.

That made 'em laugh.

Gabbitas' were the place for fireworks, bangers and jumping jacks and Roman Candles and such like. You could buy 'em in ones and twos wi' your own pocket money if you didn't spend it all on sweets first. Sometimes you just couldn't stop yoursen buying Beechnut for a penny or PK for two

24

pence and Wrigley's chewing gum an' all if you were reyt flush. If you were really rich, you could even afford a big box of Standard Fireworks, wi' a picture of rockets on the side, shooting all over the show. We never could. Some folks did though cos them big boxes used to disappear like billyo. No sooner there than gone. They couldn't have gone nowhere, could they?

Papa used to do the bonfire, it were his job - like sharpening carvin' knife wi a steel to cut joint of beef on Saturday dinner time — we could never afford chicken - all that wood broken up over his knee, and then piled up in the centre of the yard. He used to light it with paper spills from screwed up bits of newspapers. Mr Hacon gave us old beer crates to burn. They didn't half pong of stale beer, them crates. He'd just fling em down t'yard. My mother used to turn up her nose at them. She allus said beer stank. E's got beer on his breath, that's what she said of blokes, screwing up her nose. It were great, most years th'ough, Guy Fawkes night. There were hot chestnuts to eat, chuckin 'em sharpish from glove to glove cos they were red hot, and papa used to play this game he allus played with bangers. He used to light blue touch paper, drop it on the ground, and then put a bucket on it and sit on it, brazen as brass and gostering away, until BANG it went, buckin' that bucket like a horse. There were Catherine Wheels, pinned to the shed, all spinning like crazy, sparklers to run round and round with in your hand if you had gloves on, jumpin jacks zig-zagging about to run away from as fast as your legs could carry you, and Roman Candles that fizzed up into the air like coloured fountains. Pat liked Roman Candles best. She said they were beautiful, like coloured hair. Girly stuff. I were more partial to great big beautiful bangs.

We used to keep fireworks underneath our kitchen window until we had that great big disaster one year. It weren't my fault though. It were a rocket from somewhere else that came shooting up over our yard, spraying sparks. We were just laughing and pointing at first. Then something terrible started to happen to all them fireworks in cardboard boxes underneath our window that were waiting to be lit. All of a sudden, they started fizzing and banging. A jumping jack hit my leg, and I shouted and ran towards Enid's wall. I jumped up on t' dustbin and shinned ovver as fast as I could, then I scrambled up on to't dust bin on her side and watched it happening. I thought our house were goin' to go up in flames, there were that much banging an fizzing an crashing, and flames shootin' up, and Catherine wheels spinning, and jumping jacks leapin' about, and deafening bangers goin' off. I just couldn't believe it were happenin', that firework night were goin' off all at once, everything being ruined. I started cryin' an cryin'. Papa came running out of the back door and started chuckin buckets of water at it to mek it fizz an' steam. When it were all over, mum's best pot plant looked like a little shrivelled black stick, and t' kitchen window were that hot you couldn't even touch it except wi' an oven glove. Papa said he were surprised it didn't shatter. I were an all. Then, just as I were walkin back indoors, crying my eyes out, with everything ruined, biology master from our school turned up in our yard - how did he ever get to know about it? - wi' a great big box of new fireworks, and then we were all laughing again, and papa found some new wood to get that bonfire roaring up again, and we started tearing about that yard like mad eyes until mum had to drag us in kicking and screaming because it were a school night, and she didn't want us to be half asleep over our lessons next morning. Next day there were a great big black burn mark on the ground beneath our window. Made asphalt bubble. Glass were right as rain though. I touched it just to check. It's good stuff is glass. Plant pot were straight in t' dustbin though, no messin'.

This is what you would have seen if you had stood beside me on our back door step. Directly ahead of you there would be that green shed made from horizontal slats of wood. To the left of that shed, there would be the rockery from which rocks and stones would habitually fall, and where almost nothing grew out of its poor, shallow, powdery soil except for that laburnum tree which, once a year, threw down a carpet of yellow blossom. No cases of childhood poisoning were ever attributed to that fine tree. To the right of the shed stood the outside lavatories, side on to our back door, for modesty's sake. Between the shed and those lavatories there would once have been an Anderson shelter where my family and the immediate neighbours - each backyard was blessed with its own - would have huddled - half terrorised, a quarter excited - during the Sheffield Blitz, just a few years before my birth. That period of time through which you yourself do not live is called history, and to a child it can be as near or as far away as the Jurassic. And so it was with me. For me, life began in 1949. All else was supposition or make-believe.

26

Down the Gennel

Visitors to our house would enter that back yard down a gennel - a long, cool, cobbled, covered passageway between the houses. No one ever expected to enter by the street door. I liked that gennel. I liked the feel of the uneven cobbles on your feet. I enjoyed seeing the gable end of the windowless wall beyond the far end, on the other side of the street, against which I would wildly belt my football, pummelling it into submission. It never submitted. There is something exciting about the indomitability of walls. How wonderful it must have been to see the walls of Jericho fall without even being pushed by a machine!

Peering along that cool gennel — even on the hottest of summer days it was refreshingly cool - was like seeing the world through a telescope. Or down a microscope. It was a kind of thrilling, childish experiment in seeing. I would often linger in it for minutes on end, after I had been tearing up and down the street like a mad eye, killing thousands with my paper sword. Why such lingering? I was doing my best to cool down. It rarely seemed to work. I was just too profoundly overheated. No sooner did you wipe one slippery skim of salty sweat from your forehead than another layer of the stuff appeared, as if by magic. My mother hated me sweating. That's why I was always so desperate to cool down before I walked back past our kitchen window, quite casually and slowly, as if I had been doing nothing more strenuous than blow dandelion clocks into the air until you were left with nothing but that sticky, bendy hollow stem. She thought that if she caught me sweating, I would be more than likely to develop a cold. So the gennel was a handy place for doing one's best to cool a small, panting, red-faced body — there always seemed to be a fine breeze coursing through it. Goodness knows why that gennel had issued an open invitation to the breeze. I would tilt my face up to catch it, full of hope. I was always disappointed. I never managed to cool down. I was always expecting the lash of my mother's scolding words on the back door step.

My older sister Pat - we were separated in age by seven or eight years, depending upon the month of the year - had her uses for this gennel too. When she was courting Haydn, her husband-to be, they would linger — malinger more like - for minutes on end in this gennel late at night, in the dark, smooching the precious seconds away. My mother knew they were there, but there was not a thing she could do about it. All she could do was to sit in her chair, tightly gripping its arms, and imagine, and fume inwardly. Once they were indoors, also a little red-faced, I often noticed, it was a different matter altogether. She would never leave them on their own when inside the house. There would always be a very good reason not to go to bed until after Haydn had left.

You could always hear footsteps approaching our back yard, ringing down the night - or, more relaxingly, down the day. Sometimes it would be the thin, stern-faced rent man from the brewery in his trilby hat, clutching a large book - it looked more like a ledger than a book - in which he would note down payments. Or, more important, those who had failed to pay for the umpteenth time of asking. According to my mother, reminiscing many years later, when my great-grandmother had first moved into that house, the rent had been two old shillings. On more exciting occasions - for my mother at least - who never failed to appreciate the sight of a good-looking man bearing even the vaguest resemblance to Robert Mitchum - it would be the coal man. I have never quite understood why the coal man might wish to hump a sack of coal on his back all the way from the street, down our gennel, and as far as our back door when he of all people would know full well that the coal hole was directly underneath our front-room window, just a foot or so away from where his battered coal lorry would be parked. Could it have been expressly in order to flash a dazzling, white-toothed grin at my mother, who would be standing waiting to see his coal-blackened face at the back door? Whatever the reason, I have vivid memories of the coal-dust blackened face of this handsome man of medium height, good-humoured as one of those white-cane-swinging negro minstrels on the Billy Cotton Band Show, slouching past the window, cap set at a rakish angle, dragging his feet as he went. And then, perhaps once a fortnight - or perhaps when local thirst dictated - there came those two strongarms from the John Smith brewery, rolling giant wooden beer kegs, half the height of a grown man, ahead of them until they reached the very end of the gennel, at which point they would give each of these kegs a quick, deft, spin-cum-twist to the side, and align them with the chute, and then send them rolling down into the cellar of the beeroff with a tremendous, thundering trundle. These two men, late representatives from Vulcan's Smithy, wore long leather aprons, which were quite as long and as impressively flamboyant in their own way as the white aprons worn by waiters at the Brasserie Lipp in Paris, I noticed years later. I was mightily affected by these local men, and I was rendered even more puny by the sight of them approaching, bowling their mighty barrels in front of them as if they were mere playthings.

There were others who came and went too, some far too often for my mother's liking. Kitty lived half way along the road with her big, slow cat and her china cabinet, which was forever preening itself in the dark front room – why did she never open her curtains? - full of tiny, precious objects you could only ever stare at it until she took hold of your hand, quite firmly, and led you back into the kitchen. As a boy, I used to stare at the flies climbing up the wall in Kitty's kitchen. They always seemed to be walking so slowly and with such deliberation. Perhaps they liked it there. She used to hand me a rolled newspaper to bop them with. Kitty used to irritate my mother beyond measure, the way she used to pop in, so talkative and skittish, every other day, in one hat or another, always something to be said or something to be borrowed - a little pat of butter, for example, not so willingly handed over. There was no one quite so devoted to her daily routines as Kitty. On a Tuesday she would be carefully washing the huge leaves of the aspidistra plant that used to grow in a giant blue ceramic pot in her front window, and then on a Wednesday she would be sitting out on the ledge of the first floor window facing the street, carefree as Buster Keaton in his white panama, leaning out far enough to make you want to bite your nails, winding round and round with a cloth until the panes gleamed. The worst thing about her was to do with money and how she hoarded it. She had so much of it, and she barely spent any of it. She didn't trust banks though. Not many people trusted banks along Coningsby Road. She put all her money underneath the bed, and after she died her only relative, a nephew who looked older and much more wheezy than Kitty herself, dragged it all out, mouth watering, only to discover that it was all out of date, all those ten shillings notes lovingly held together by old, long-perished rubber bands.

In the Kitchen

Each room in a small house has its own recognisable character. The smaller the house, the more intensely you feel about its spaces. 45 Coningsby Road had six such spaces: the kitchen, the front room, the front bedroom, the much smaller back bedroom, the attic and the cellar. The kitchen, which opened out directly into the back yard, was the most used room of the house. It was also the smallest. It was in this tiny, overheated room that the dramas of the house were played out, where the major arguments were staged, where all the meals were cooked and taken, and the washing done. All human life was there. It was also where the wireless lorded it over us, on a high shelf above the table, in the absolute control of my grandfather. It was my grandfather who switched on the news at one and the news at six, and then switched it off again. It was my grandfather who stood sternly by, ear cocked, as we listened to a dramatic tale of tanks rolling into Prague in 1968. It was that radio which, on a Sunday morning, would play me some of my favourite, silly childhood songs - The Laughing Policeman, Archie the Talking Piano, How Much Is That Doggie in the Window? The answer to that last question was always the same: too much. I was never allowed to have a dog, no matter how many times I rolled around the floor, impotently pummelling the carpet with my fists and thrashing my legs. I had to make do with small pets instead that lasted two years or less. Rubbish.

My grandfather was always the mediator in all these radio matters. He was our portal to the world's news. And it was in this kitchen where the television would first come to live too, when one eventually arrived in the house, together with all the coming excitement of The Billy Cotton Band Show — *Wakey, Wakey!* shouted the big man in glasses and dicky bow, clapping his hands – and Morecambe and Wise, the funniest men that God had ever invented. Even to think of Eric Morecambe pulling his glasses side-on half way down his face still makes me laugh out loud. The arrival of that television, with its screen scarcely bigger than an over-size shoe box, must have happened when I was about ten years old. Until then I would watch television at a neighbour's. I remember so well being mesmerised by the sight of traffic, a tumult of cars and buses and taxis, circling and circling Piccadilly Circus before the beginning of the six o'clock news bulletin.

Yes, this kitchen was unlike any other room of that house. Everything of any moment happened there, and the single most important reason for this was quite simple: it was heated. It is difficult to describe quite how cold and damp a house could feel before the era of central heating. Heating brings comfort and optimism and a sense of well being in its wake. It bonds human beings. It enables them to relax in each other's company. It gives meaning to the idea of leisure. We lived in that kitchen. I did my school essays on our dining table. We even took baths there.

The bathing ritual took place on a Thursday evening. It was prolonged and elaborate. It necessitated the boiling of many kettles and pans of hot water on the stove. It also required the willing help of my grandfather or my uncle. They would heave the long, heavy, scratchy zinc bath up from the cellar – I could hear it bonging against the walls as it was carried up the cellar steps - and plonk it down on top of the hand-made flock rug beside the open fire. Then there would be the wooden clothes horse to be fetched, which would be used to create a kind of wooden palisade in front of the open fire. Blankets and towels would be hung from the clothes horse for privacy's sake. And then, when the various buckets and kettles of hot and cold water had been poured in, the lucky bather would step into the bath and, as he splashed around for minutes on end, he would stare into the raging fire. It felt so wonderful to be there, with blankets hung at your back to screen off any draughts, and a warming fire in your face, so cosy and so enveloping. After the first lucky bather had vacated the tub – mum would fling a towel around my shivering person and start violently rubbing and rubbing - a second would be invited in: my sister. A bit of extra hot water would be added for good measure. If there was whitish scum floating on the surface, so be it. This was not the Ritz. (Who'd ever heard of The Ritz?) It was bath night at 45 Coningsby Road.

Keeping clean(ish) was not a problem for children alone, of course. What did the adults do? I became acutely conscious of this need to find a bath somewhere – anywhere - when I grew a little older. We (my uncle, my grandfather and I) became bath-seeking wanderers, moving back and forth across the city, rolled bath towels tucked into our armpits, seeking hot water in a tub. Any welcoming tub would do. Even warmish water would do. The first stop might by the Scunthorpe Road Public Baths at Pitsmoor where I was taken as a child with the rest of our raucous school party, wild kids soaking each other amidst the frenzy and the mayhem of splashy water. How voices do echo in a swimming baths! Upstairs from that rather grim and institutionalised public pool where I learnt my life-long fear of swimming – a sadistic swimming instructor called Mr Scott once forced me to jump in before I could swim, and that feeling of flailing about underwater, imagining that I was drowning, terrorised me then and forever after - there was an entire floor of what were called slipper baths. These were huge marble tubs, twice the size of ours at Coningsby Road, with giant, gleaming brass taps which positively gushed unlimited amounts of hot and cold water. My grandfather and I would go together, each with his own separate towel.

Or we could profit by the fact that when my grandfather retired from being a groundsman at Crimicar Lane, he took an administrative job with the same institution at its headquarters in Fargate. I would go there on a Thursday night with my Uncle Ken, first of all climbing the longest set of stairs up to my grandfather's office that I had ever seen in my life. That set of wide stone steps, as monumental to the eyes of a child as the steps that lead up to the main concourse of the Mussolini-era Central Station in Milan, added enormously to the sense of adventure. We would bathe in a tub, and then play billiards and table tennis in the sports hall. After which there would be warming cups of tea from one of the YMCA's huge aluminium kettles, brewed and served by my grandfather. I used to explore the back rooms of the YMCA on bath night, peering into dark and dusty rooms and leafing through huge old ledgers with marble-edged pages. These ledgers were full of figures, what dead man had paid for what and when. The lovely handwriting always looked so important.

But what did the women – my mother and my grandmother, for example – do for washing? There was an arcane practice called 'strip-washing' which I often heard and thought about but, unsurprisingly, never witnessed. This would have involved, I am sure, standing in front of the kitchen sink, removing various – all? surely not - layers of clothing, and then, somehow, washing the parts that were usually invisible to the ever curious eyes of a child. But how much really ever got washed, and with what degree of thoroughness? No adult could have climbed into our old butler's sink. One leg would have almost overfilled it. I remember once walking into my mother's bedroom and staring down at her pillow slip. The bed was unmade. I could see the imprint of her large head in the pillow. The pillow slip was shockingly greasy and stained brown with the hair colouring she used. I recoiled in horror at the sight of it. She had no one to wash her hair for - until that carpet layer from Liverpool brought about a change in her fortunes after I had left home for university. Yes, later on that pillow slip of hers was always clean.

Strange things happened to me in that Coningsby Road kitchen, though the naked eye would not necessarily have registered them. If you wish to become a writer, you do find yourself rejecting who and what you are at a certain point in your life - even if you half-know that you are sure to return to the same preoccupations later. This has nothing to do with snobbery, disgust with one's family or disapproval of one's social circumstances. It is something far odder and more subtle. It is something to do with an inward need to liberate the inner self from the regular circumstances of the everyday, to live and to breathe in an entirely different atmosphere. This happened to me at least twice during my teenage years. It happened for the first time when religion seized hold of me one windswept evening in a tent on an island just off the coast of North Wales, and transported me to regions of the mind that I had never before seen, regions inhabited by gods and their attendant systems of belief, that I scarcely knew existed until that moment. It happened for the second time in the kitchen at Coningsby Road, when I was about sixteen years old. It was one evening in winter. The lights were blazing. There was the usual noise and bustle. That kitchen, as ever, felt like an intersection of busy roads. I remember that I had in my hand a fat yellow book by a poet of the French Renaissance called Pierre Ronsard. I had just been reading it upstairs. I came down with it in my hand. My head was still full of the vocabulary of this sixteenth-century poet. I could hear the music of his words ringing in my ears. I looked around. No one else was a privy to what I was thinking or feeling or rehearsing over to myself in the private chambers of my mind. I remember feeling a tremendous sense of secret pleasure at that thought, that I was both standing there, in the bosom of my family, and that I was utterly elsewhere too, being inwardly nourished by something utterly strange and unimaginable to everyone at whom I was smiling. Is this memory repulsive or shameful? Was I sickeningly elitist to be experiencing such hidden pleasures?

There were three doors that opened off that kitchen, all panelled when I was little, and all modern and flushed and painted a rather sickly, cold beige by the 1960s. When I was a little boy, doors had knobs that turned. Later, after all the so-called improvements, it became even easier to open a door. Knobs disappeared. Finicky plastic handles were put on, and tiny little ball bearings set into the door frame, so you could shock people by just pushing, and then coming in at an almighty rush, shouting. Only if you felt like it though. The door diagonally opposite the outside door led down to the cellar. I really liked that cellar.

The Cellar

The steps down to that cellar were cold, damp-feeling and a bit uneven. You grazed the top of your head as you went down. A skim of plaster dust on your sister's hair when she steps into the kitchen from the cellar steps can look quite comical. It positively reeked of damp, that cellar, and the walls were peeling whitewash.

All sorts of stuff was kept down there, things you didn't really want any more, but just couldn't bear to part with just yet, and really useful stuff as well like the big zinc bath for bath night. My grandmother Mabel's mother used to take washing in during the 1930s to help her get by. She wasn't supposed to, but she did. The bad woman at the beeroff told on her once to the brewery bloke, and she nearly lost the house. The old wash tub she used for all that towing and squeezing was still down there – it wasn't half bad as a drum if you bashed it quite hard with a stick, especially in that echoey place. Then, reared up behind it against the wall, there was the washboard that you rubbed clothes against to get all the dirt out, rubbing and drubbing until you were red in the face. I never saw that washboard being used for clothes, but I remember Lonnie Donegan and his skiffle group using one as a musical instrument after we got a telly, going up and down it with his finger ends hell-for-leather to set up a scratchy-sounding rhythm. That was worth trying. More boring than a drum though. Then there was the old mangle with its two fierce rubber rollers that my mother caught her finger in once. That's why she always had a funny squashed finger, crushed like a bit of squeezed up pastry before you cook it. I remember the sight of heavy, wet blankets being folded between my mother and my grandmother, and how they would stand apart from each other, arms raised, holding up the ends, and then walk towards each other, and fold over, and, slowly raising their arms, let ends touch ends with their finger ends. It looked like a strange dance, that performance on wash day.

That finger wasn't the only funny thing about the way my mother looked. She had a cast in her eye, which meant that one eye didn't look straight ahead. It was lazy, she told me. How could an eye be lazy though? Much later on, I saw from my mother's wedding photograph that my father had one too. They were both standing in front of a giant, tiered wedding cake in a little front room, thin as whistles, wearing these great big glasses. The glasses were the biggest things about them. She also had a brown tooth at the very front that got browner as she got older. It was dead, I was told when I enquired. How did a tooth die though? The cast in her eye meant that she had to wear glasses all her life. That tooth never did anything but change colour, getting darker and darker as if it were night coming on, very gradually. In fact, her teeth didn't go all pleasingly white again until she acquired a proper set of smart false ones, and that was much later on, after she'd married for a second time. They both did it together, she and Wilf Welsby. There was no shame about false teeth. No one expected teeth to live forever. In fact, false ones were so much better, they always said, so much less of a botheration. You just popped them into a jam jar of cloudy water when you wanted to relax your jaws a bit. It did make you talk and look a bit funny though when you left them out, as if your face had half-collapsed. Best to keep them in for company. Sometimes she didn't.

In the corner of the cellar next to the street, there was the coal hole. You could always see chinks of light - little, thin shafts of it, not that much - beaming down from outdoors if you scrabbled up the coal heap and peered up. That corner was always heaped up with coal, gleaming black nuggets or big lumps of it that came off on your hand when you picked it up to toss it from hand to hand. It didn't half make a mess of your clothes. You got into right trouble if you picked it up, and then just forgot where you were putting your fingers. I often climbed it, that big heap. Tried to, more like. You slipped back as you ran up. The coalman used to whip a sack of it off the lorry onto his shoulder, and then empty it down our coal hole — as I've said, you could see the light of the street, just a chink through the grate, if you leant under the coal hole and looked up the chute. You used to hear it coming down when they did the delivery, like thunder rumbling and tumbling, making the kitchen floor tremble a bit. It were a bit of a bother, fetching and carrying that coal up from the cellar to the kitchen, especially in winter when you never wanted the fire in the grate to go out or you'd practically freeze to death, no matter how many times you blew on your fingers or hopped about on one leg to keep warm. Sometimes you envied the toast on the end of that metal toasting fork with its prongy ends.

Then there was Harold's rough old work bench, all pitted and bashed about from hammering and sawing and such like, with that big metal vice attached to the edge of it. I loved that vice. It had a long, thick metal handle you used to wind and wind as you watched the jaws of the vice getting closer and closer. Sometimes you dared yourself to leave your finger in it. In addition to all the tools, I kept wooden cages containing small animals on that bench. One year it would be hamsters, the next mice or guinea pigs. There is nothing quite like the feel of a small slippery white mouse doing quick acrobatics through your fingers. Best not to drop them, though they seldom seemed to mind much if you did. One of the worst days of my young life was when my hamster Timmy had six babies. I knew there were six because I uncovered them in the nest - they were like writhing, flesh-coloured jelly babies, noses sniffing the air, blind as bats. By the next morning Timmy had eaten them. Never pry into mother's nests.

The Front Room

If you had opened the door which separated the kitchen from the bottom of the stairs, you would have seen another door, just beyond the overloaded coat pegs you could always hide behind for a game, which led into the front room. This was the room which overlooked the street, the front room, the room reserved for best. Best of what though? Best of almost nothing. Very little happened in this room until I was a teenager. At that point a gas fire replaced the old fire grate, and the grandmother clock - a wedding present for my mother - which had always stood in the corner, and which was the closest this house ever came to owning an object of value that, in future years, might even mature into an antique, moved upstairs onto the landing outside my uncle's back bedroom. That clock sits in my sister's house in Holymoorside now, proudly maturing away. Like the bedrooms, this front room was miserably unheated, and therefore uninhabited for the most part when I was very small.

Except on social occasions. At Christmas, hazel nuts and walnuts and brazil nuts, all patiently waiting to be cracked open, would appear in a special bowl on a small side table, together with the nutcrackers, so that my grandfather could do his manly work of cracking them open. One of his other manly jobs, as I think I've already mentioned, was to expertly carve every joint of beef that ever entered the house to make slices thin enough to see the light through. There would also be a box of dates, and a bottle of sherry. This bottle of sherry never cut much of a dash. I felt that it was there on sufferance, as a nod in the general direction of what usually happened, in most families, at this time of year. My mother Dorothy wholly disapproved of drink, and I seldom saw anyone actually opening this bottle or sampling the dangerous stuff. I do not remember it ever being surrounded by sherry glasses either. What were sherry glasses any road? It merely stood there, a stiff, defiant, ever present testimony to the fact that, well, this was Christmas, wasn't it, and any great feast such as this one generally entailed a modicum of alcohol.

And then there was the old upright piano, Dorothy's world. On the top of this piano, at the far end on the left - I can still nearly touch it - there would be the special Christmas trifle in a high-sided, circular, faceted glass bowl, inches deep with tinned strawberries and tinned mandarins and custard, all mixed up together, and topped with thickly foaming whipped cream. Looking through the thick glass of that bowl, down and down through the various layers of deliciousness, was a bit like swimming underwater, open-eyed, at the sea side. Except that trifle tastes a thousand times more delicious than salty sea water, ugh.

Yes, if there was any ritual in that house, any rite which brought us together - and there was very little - it pivoted about the old upright piano, which Dorothy had been taught to play from childhood on, and which had been brought down from Crimicar Lane. And how she did play on these occasions! Never for very long though. It would not have done to go on for too long. The sheet music would be kept inside the piano stool on which she sat, and out it would come, each double page spread held open on its fragile wooden rack attached to the back of the piano, with tiny spikes of metal that swung from side to side - if you made them do it - like car windscreen wipers. Dorothy would play her favourites - Chopin's waltzes or Rachmaninov - with tremendous gushes of emotion, flinging her arms up and down the keyboard with uncharacteristic abandon, almost frightening in its intensity. It was as if, at last, she was being swept up into the romantic cinematic dream of a lifetime, some yearned for tryst with Robert Mitchum, as far away from the humdrumness and the dreariness of Coningsby Road as it was humanly possible to be. We would all sit there, marvelling. Kenneth would be hunched slightly forward, gently stroking his moustaches or, from time to time, sniffing at his nicotine-stained finger ends. He was a bit of a smoker in those days. Not later though. Dorothy always played the same tunes, in exactly the same way, and we always marvelled at her, and clapped her furiously when she had finished. And she always laughed, quite flightily, quite dismissively too, as we did so, as if to say: there's loads more where that came from, but you're not necessarily getting it.

What else was there in this room? Precious little. I remember it as featureless, odourless, a place generally lacking in human love and human attention. There was a built in cupboard beneath the window which, when opened, smelt powerfully of damp. It was here that we kept, unloved, neglected, the only book which contained photographs of works of art I ever remember having been in that house. It was quite a grand book, red and leather-bound, large in format, but its cover and its damp, ripply-warped pages smelled of mildew. Occasionally, intrigued by its presence there, I would leaf through its pages, some half glued together by the damp, of black-and white reproductions of sentimental Victorian narrative scenes. The world of art seemed so sad and so old-timey distant.

And then, at a certain point in the early 1960s, the character of that front room changed. It was no longer the cold place it had always been, set apart, seldom visited, used on ceremonial occasions only. What made all the difference? Gas and television. A gold-coloured gas fire was installed with a gridded front through which you poked, at about seven o'clock in the evening, and even earlier if you wished to catch the evening news, sputtering Captain Webb Safety Matches while, simultaneously, twisting the metal key in the centre of the gas pipe that snaked along, dangerously, at floor level. All of a sudden, it would flame up and out with a mighty roaring BOOMF, and you would jump back, instantly warmed if not scorched - and delighted. What an astonishing thing this was, instant heat that could be turned on or off at a metal tap! And then, as if encouraged by the prospect of comfort, there also arrived a big, saggily comfy sofa in front of which to enjoy a small, heavy television, with a twelve-inch screen, which would give us programmes until such time as they stopped, quite abruptly, and we all stood up, stretching and yawning, with Uncle Ken looking at his watch, which he always wore facing the inside of his wrist. And then he would turn it off, and we would all watch the display shrink down to a tiny, mesmerising white dot. One of the favourite rituals of my later teenage years was now in place, to sit there with my family, all happily bunched up together in the semi-dark, and watch Steptoe and Son, Hancock's Half Hour and Brian Rix's farces beamed directly to us, in north-east Sheffield, from the Whitehall Theatre, London. Marvels indeed.

The Staircase

A staircase can be a mighty presence in a house. And so it was at 45 Coningsby Road. The staircase led up from the ground floor, with its hot, busy kitchen and cold, seldom occupied front room, to the two bedrooms on the first floor. (There was a second short flight, a twisty affair, which ascended from the first floor to the attic.) It was long, this staircase - twelve tall steps - and very steep. I associate this staircase with unhappy events. This was the staircase down which the body of my grandmother was carried in a wicker armchair by two strong men from the Funeral Directors after she died of pneumonia in the front bedroom at the age of seventy-four. The mind plays tricks when you think back to the past, confusing real happenings with fantasy, embellishing the real. I feel that I can still remember standing beside her body as she lay dying in bed. I am leaning over her, listening with horror-struck fascination as she repeats the Lord's Prayer over to herself - backwards. I have repeated that story over to myself, many times. I have never shared it with anyone else - until now - because it always felt too eerily troubling. But does this vivid recollection mean that it was true?

After her death, she was brought down those stairs so awkwardly, covered in a sheet, bumpingly, step by step. I watched it happen. I saw those big men wrestling with the wicker armchair in which her body lay, doing their best to prevent it falling out. It did not fall out. I had not until then thought of a human being as so much lumber, akin to a plank of wood or a beer barrel. I remember lying awake that night, thinking about that hard and clumsy descent, and trying to feel the upset that my sobbing sister Pat was feeling. I remember instead feeling a terrible shocked hollowness, but nothing else at all akin to upset. Some part of me couldn't prevent myself finding the descent of her body slightly ridiculous.

The second tragedy, the fall of my grandfather Harold down that same staircase, from top to bottom, when he was a very old man, was reported to me by my mother some days after it had happened. She told me of the sounds he was making as he lay there in a crumpled heap at the foot of the stairs, the terrible gagging noises. He had swallowed his tongue. I have no doubts that Harold's fall hastened his death. And so the idea of those stairs has dark connotations for me, hints of menace and fear.

Not so with the bedrooms and the attic. As far as sleeping arrangements were concerned, I, being the youngest, the most biddable, and the most easily transportable, was something of an itinerant in that house.

It was a little like a game of musical chairs. When the music stopped, I would wake up in a different bed, in a different room altogether.

The Front Bedroom

As a very small child I slept in the front bedroom facing the street because I remember my cot being squeezed up against the street wall, and Dorothy's face reading to me from a big fat omnibus of children's stories when the bars were down. What intrigued me most was the way, when cars passed by at nights, which wasn't very often, yellow lights would come raking and combing across the ceiling. I remember that room best for the fact that I used to cry in it, night after night, helplessly marooned in my bed. I couldn't stop myself thinking about my mother dying. There was a tall, rangy weed with white flowers that we used to call mother's die. It seemed to grow everywhere, beside the road, in the allotments, wherever it saw half a chance to flourish. I never touched the stuff. I always hurried past it, only half-looking. Rose bay willow herb is its name. Now that I know its botanical name, I can establish a degree of emotional distance between it and me.

That arrangement soon changed though. For most of my early life the front bedroom was where my grandparents Harold and Mabel slept in their big, solid bed which blocked off most of the room, and so not a lot of my time was spent there. No one would have approved too much if I had spent much time in my grandparents' bedroom. There was a big, dark, built-in closet in the corner where old things were stored – I remember finding umpteen copies of my sister's *Photoplay* lovingly bound up in string, with its pictures of knock-kneed film stars in swimsuits on the cover. I also stored my second-hand zither there, one of the many musical instruments I bought from the swap shops down Owler Lane way, and even as far as Attercliffe.

They were called swap shops, but they weren't really about swapping, though you could take things back there and get some money off your next purchase. No, they were really about buying exciting second-hand things pretty cheaply. The best swap shops were in Attercliffe. But the one I liked best (because it was the nearest) was quite close to the end of Osgathorpe Road, and it was run by Dennis in his greasy overcoat, and his sideburns, and his long, leaning, nosy-seeming body. The windows of these places, which were always flooded with yellow light, and noisy, exciting, hand-made, buy-me-now signs in the shape of stars, were positively stuffed with second-hand cameras and knives and air pistols and pellet guns and aluminium catapults and such like. I adored buying bone-handled, long-bladed knives with long and fiercesome blades. No one ever stopped me. My mother never complained. I kept them in drawers, to look at, in private. I had them there for when I would need them. The truth is that I never really needed them. Things never got that bad. I didn't murder a single enemy. I loved that zither too because once you'd tuned the strings relative to each other, it was the easiest instrument to play in the world. To get a lovely sounding chord wafted all the way to Coningsby Road from the Appalachian Mountains, all you had to do was to press down on the pearly little stops on the black wooden keys. Later on, the guitar became my first love, and I managed to persuade my church friend Tony Dale to sell me his newly purchased Framus twelve-string for £9. Goodness knows why he let me have it for so little. I think it was because he had, within weeks of buying his twelve-string, become besotted by the Vibraphone – Tony changed instruments as fast as other people changed coats when the weather switches from hot to cold. And so a Framus twelve-string it was to be, life-long, and I quickly learnt to play it, with brash carelessness, back to front because I am left-handed - a friend at church even switched the finger board around - teaching myself the rudimentaries of the craft with the aid of Bert Weedon's Guitar Manual, and learning my extensive Western folknik's repertoire of twenty to thirty songs from the Woody Guthrie Songbook. Regrettably, I clean forgot to switch the strings round, so I continue to play the thing upside down to this day. The next trick - a step too far for my perverse ingenuity - would have been to learn to sing the songs of Bob Dylan backwards.

And then there was the tallboy, where I found a few books, grandfather's big pocket watch in the topmost drawer - still working if you wound it, but not too much or you'd risk breaking it - and some strange device whose use was never clear to me, which consisted of long lengths of brown rubber tubing attached to what looked like a squeezy pump of sorts. Some form of primitive medical apparatus, I decided, though I never asked, and I never saw it used, thank goodness. And then, in the other top drawer, carefully wrapped in old paper, there was that strange, heavy, hard-headed ceramic doll with its funny loose and gangly limbs, its grubby canvas neck, and its very slowly blinking eyes if you tilted the head in the right direction, and had the patience to wait for a moment. Otherwise, it just stared and stared at you. When you picked it up, the head would loll forwards, terribly, as if it had just then decided to fall asleep in order to annoy you because it knew you'd just picked it up to wake it up. This old doll may or may not have belonged to my mother. No one ever claimed it. No one ever paid it the slightest bit of attention but me.

As a tiny child, I slept in a single bed up in the attic. My sister and my mother slept in the same room in those earliest childhood days, in a double bed, with an extraordinarily saggy and squeaky mattress, just inches away from me. It is difficult to conjure up the coldness of that attic bedroom, and almost physically painful to remember what misery you suffered when you eventually persuaded your shivering body to leap out of bed in the morning, and then snatched at clothes, strewn here and there in the dark, to hide your puny, shivering nakedness. The big double bed which contained my sister and mother was just beside me, where I would listen to large forms heaving and sighing and tossing far into the night. My mother, life-long, complained of being a bad sleeper, as if this were a heroic affliction of which we should all be particularly proud. Many years later, my sister and I recommended that she apply for a job as a night watchman. We laughed until our faces practically fell off.

The Back Bedroom

The back bedroom overlooked our back yard. It was the smallest, most featureless and most sparsely furnished room of the entire house, and it was my Uncle Ken's bedroom. For a couple of years before he left the house as a married man, I shared that bedroom with him. We slept in two tiny single beds, with a narrow corridor of space down the middle. Underneath his bed there was a chamber pot into which he would urinate, quietly, with the utmost discretion, back always turned to me, in the middle of the night. The walls were completely unadorned, and I remember a tiny trickle of books on the bedside table, the most memorable being a hardback edition of the *Collected Poems* of Rupert Brooke, bound in green. Occasionally I would read this book. I became especially fond of Brooke's sentimental sonnet about the First World War, in which he imagines his own heroism in battle as a representative English soldier, and everything that this would come to represent in the years to come. The stirring sentimentality of his words ennobled him in my eyes. It was not until some years later that I discovered he had died somewhat ignominiously, of an infection, before even reaching the field of battle. The heroics were so much shadow-boxing. Not once did I ever make a link between Brooke's soaring words and my grandfather's terrible experiences at the Somme.

And then, all of a sudden - at least, that is how it seemed to me - I became the sole occupant of that back bedroom. When I was sixteen years old, my uncle got married to Auntie Ena, and he moved to her first-floor flat in a much more salubrious part of the city. The discovery of this flat of hers was something of a marvel to me. I'd never seen anything like it. It was a bit like a tiny snippet of a stately home. It was so richly carpeted - the soles of your feet felt strangely soothed by the pile of the carpet when you walked across the sitting-cum-dining room. The entire interior had a strange, polite hush about it. Meals were taken ritualistically. Everything - each plate, every crust of bread - had its appointed place, and woe betide you if, knowingly or not, you should shift it from that place. It unnerved me and my mother. We felt ourselves to be awkward, uncouth blunderers within the refined and tranquil fastness of that flat, with its oil paintings of local landscapes - a bridge over a stream, a farmhouse set in some bosky glade - by the noted Eddie Billen (Auntie Ena's brother-in-law) on the walls. It was as if we felt ourselves, always, to be on the brink of doing something that would be judged to be impolite or mildly distasteful. Socially, we were not quite up to scratch in such a refined and tranquil interior. And yet Auntie Ena, as she carried selected items of her family silver to the table, or slightly re-arranged the beautiful table mats, remained unfailingly polite and kind to us. What is more - and this was perhaps the most wonderful aspect of that flat - she gave us permission to carry our own rolled bath towels across the city, and to bathe in her own bath tub in the small, indoor bathroom. This was special indeed. This was social refinement on a scale hitherto unglimpsed. How pampered and perfumed, how deliciously relaxed and raised up I always felt after bathing in that room of hers for just as long as it took me, wallowing in warm water and dreaming the minutes away! Oh yes, I was so careful not to splash. I even dusted myself down with a bit of her pink talcum powder just to see what it felt like.

One thing was evident to me. Uncle Ken himself seemed very happy there. It was as if this was the kind of sequestered spot for which he had always been looking. He played a part in all the small rituals of that place with ease. He had found a home for himself. And it was no longer the house that was still home for me. He had moved on.

After Uncle Ken's departure, I inherited that back bedroom in its entirety. I pinned my maps to the walls, just the two of them, and, at nights, in the year or so that remained to me before the great fall from grace, I knelt beside the bed where my uncle had once slept, and prayed that I might be protected from the temptations that were now assailing me from every direction.

The Attic

Years later, after my Uncle Ken and my sister had married, I inherited the attic room. It became my eyrie, the place where I could discover the person that I was slowly becoming. A new door was put in at the bottom of the short, twisty staircase which led up from the middle landing to make it feel even more separate from the rest of the house. An entire wall of book shelving was built, and rapidly filled with godly literature. The only window was a skylight, which gave onto a prospect of warring grey sky on most days. The din of the oxyacetylene torches sounded particularly rasping through this window. One day I found a small, flattish fragment of metal out in the street, no bigger than the palm of a hand, which replicated almost exactly the shape of the head of a bird with a violently prodding beak. This metal sculpture, I recognised, was worthy of prolonged contemplation. I drove the pronged end of its base into the window sill of the skylight. That metal bird became a kind of sentinel, keeping watch over me when I was sleeping. What is more, there was a cubby hole directly beneath that skylight into which a chair could be fitted. That became a favourite reading spot. For the walls of the room itself, I chose wallpaper of a particularly dark and swirling blue, which drew that small space in, making it feel thrillingly confined and confining. I lay on my bed during the day quite frequently, reading Shelley's 'Adonais', dreaming my way into moods of hypersensitivity and delicious set apartness, incubating my future self.

Like all houses everywhere, 45 Coningsby Road changed with the years and the prevailing fashions. The old, rolled-top secretaire, once pride of the kitchen, having outlived its usefulness, was hauled out into the back yard and chopped up for fire wood. The old, labouresomely hand-made flock rug that hid squirming silver fish by the dozen if you were unwise enough to lift up one of its edges, was thrown out too. A new shelf, almost at ceiling height, was attached to the wall, with sturdy brackets to accommodate the newish second-hand radio. Old, panelled doors were flushed (covered with plain sheets of plywood) and then painted a fashionable beige to make them look up-to-the-minute. I never liked that colour. It always felt cold to me. The open fire, so wonderful for cooking toast on the prongs of the old toasting fork, made way for a gas fire. And, everywhere about that house, my mother proved to be a dab hand at the wallpapering, flinging long lengths out down the ironing board, lathering them with thick white paste, and then smoothing them out flat against the wall, top to bottom, with the aid of a long-handled sweeping brush.

Street Scene

There was the back yard and then, legs racing quickly down the gennel, there was the street, Coningsby Road itself, a continuous run of terraced housing of about 150 metres in length with a slight kink in the middle. Every house was like every house. Every chimney sent up the same wavering spume of dirty smoke when autumn set in. In spite of this undeniable fact, my mother was quick to register social differences, tiny reasons to feel mildly superior. The inhabitants of our end of the street, for example, were of a more elevated social status than the rougher families who lived at the far end, where the street met Barnsley Road. She knew that by their eating habits. When they bought take-away dinners from the Sunbeam Fish Bar just around the corner from the end of the street, they would always buy, she told me, fish cakes - breaded fish mixed with potato - and not battered cod (or haddock) and chips. This meant, according to my mother, two quite different things. That they were too undiscerning to recognise the superior value of fish unmixed with potato, and that they were too poor to buy fish and chips. Two very good reasons to have nothing to do with them. We kept our distance.

How do you begin to memorialise the past? I ask myself that question again and again as I stare into our old backyard and remember those neighbours of ours whose back doors also opened out into it. There was kindly and slow-moving Mrs Whitworth, for example, whose daughter was as lean, hollow-eyed and nervy as her mother was fresh-faced, slow-moving and cuddly-corpulent. 'She's scrattin' herself to death, that one,' said my mother one day, and it seemed to be true. Mrs Whitworth's daughter was forever looking for things to clean: steps, windows, curtains, flower pots. Mrs Whitworth was the third person to live in that house next to ours during the years that I lived there. The first occupants, a family of four, left for Canada when I was about eight years old. They sent me back cartoon supplements from the Canadian newspapers, long, thick scrolls of them. That was some of the most exciting post I ever received. After them came Johnny Heath who drove a swanky sports car whose windscreen got smashed by flying roof tiles during one day of ferocious winds in 1962. Johnny Heath brought with him a huge and not so fearsome alsatian, Dino. Dino used to sit in the front window facing the street, waiting for his master to return. When he saw Johnny approaching, he would throw himself at the window.

Then one day one of Johnny's windows really did get smashed. Not by Dino though. I'd been playing in our back yard, flinging a tennis ball up against the wall between our window and his, harder and harder, for sheer dare-devilry's sake. When the sickening crash happened, Johnny flew out of his door like a madder version of his own dog, and started shouting at me. My mother flung open our back door in her turn and positively flew at him. He hadn't reckoned on such a sudden and wholly unmerited counter-attack from a woman who could be even more ferocious than a wild dog when her precious son was being subjected to a verbal savaging. I was astonished by this. I didn't say much though. I just flew indoors, settled down on the kitchen sofa where I used to lie and dream when I was too ill to go to school, and started reading a book about Custer's Last Stand.

On the other side of our house there was the home of Mrs Aidy, a big-boned woman in a pinny who seemed to possess the strength of several men. During the 1970s, when I worked as a children's books' editor, I began to write little poems about some of these people. They were written in the voice of an amazed and slightly over-awed child. One of these poems described this next-door neighbour of ours, her commanding presence, her singular eating habits, and her ever tempestuous relationship with her own daughter.

Mrs Aidy wasn't exactly
what my mother'd call a lady.
All she ever had to fill her insides
was a packet of fags, and vinegar sandwiches
in bread as thick as a house side.
But was she some strong!
She once lifted me straight through their window
When her daughter locked her out in a temper.
But that was the least we had to sort out.
They'd lob the dinner plates when they really got going,
and once, after one of them had sent the other flying off a chair,
my mother found Mrs Aidy coming to
at the bottom of the cellar stairs.
I think she deserved all she got.
After all, would you take it sitting down
if your mother kept the kettle on the hob
just for the pleasure of steaming open
your sweetheart's letters
so that she'd something to fill her gossipy gob?

Is all this true? I heard a lot of it for myself, the shouting and the smashing of dinner plates when they fought like cat and dog around their kitchen. And Mrs Aidy certainly lifted me straight through her window, easy as pie, when I was a small boy. She'd locked herself out, the silly woman. What is more, she treated Majorie's young man much more spitefully than Dorothy ever treated my sister's Haydn. Once, according to my mother, Mrs Aidy lay full length in front of the cooker to stop Marjorie preparing food for her husband-to-be.

There were those who lived in our backyard, and then there were the neighbours who regularly passed by, the ones, for example, who were making their regular pilgrimage to the beeroff on the corner. I've already mentioned Kitty. Mrs Lockin was my favourite, ambling so slowly along in her blue pinafore, head in curlers, house slippers slipping off her feet, with a white jug grasped firmly in her fist, ready to be filled up with stout foaming to the brim.

In 1964, bang in the middle of my phase of religious mania, Billy Graham, that televangelist beloved of American presidents, came to England with his army of eager young crusaders. Sheffield's evangelical community worked itself up into a frenzy of excitement as we plotted how to nurture newly saved souls. The services were shown on giant screens in the City Hall. Some years later, I imagined Mrs Lockin being converted by Billy in 1964, and swilling all her bad habits down the drain. And, into the bargain, mounting a bicycle for the greater good of her health.

Mrs Lockin's jumped on Billy's gospel train,
Fags in the dustbin and drink down the drain!
Hands off the mincer and up with the blind.
Pedal the fat off your great behind!

I loved the corner shop on the end of our street which doubled as a beeroff, the magic of what went on behind the counter to which children, standing expectantly on the wrong side of it, were never privy, that feeling of sickening jealousy directed at the children of the shopkeeper's family, with their god-given right to wander into the back of the shop when the mood seized them, and snatch a sweet or two or a packet of crisps or a Dairy Milk Flake... It was run by Mrs Hacon, bouncy as a ball and giggly-friendly. I used to go in for two ounces of chopped pork, thinly sliced, in greaseproof paper, to eat out in the street. She always used to give me extra. At the back of the shop were their living quarters, with the tiny TV where I first watched Pop Eye, swelling his muscles by pouring spinach from the can straight down his throat like a mighty, curving torrent of water.

That batch of children's poems about my childhood came all of a rush. They gave me sudden, fleeting glimpses of my early teenage years, when I would travel into town on the bus on a Saturday morning, and walk around the new, elevated walkway beside Woolworth's, round and round and round, with the collar of my green sloppily casual jacket turned up at a dangerous angle, dreaming about girls, in the grip of something unstoppable, uncontainable, unmanageable. And even occasionally descending to the lower ground floor of Woolworth's itself where they sold poor, cheap cover versions of the latest pop hits – you always knew them by the red labels at the centre of the record - looking out for a lustful returned glance rather than a giggle behind the hand. But girls, unlike me, were hardly ever on their own. When I spotted them, they always seemed to be rolling about in pairs, arm in arm, acting daft and gostering. So this next little poem strikes me as a bit of a fantasy.

Woolworth's was always a favourite patch of mine.
You could usually count on some piece smiling
round about the nylons.
The trouble was how to take it from there.
You could hardly make out you were
her father or lover
with a hawk-eyed little brother.
Usually, you'd write down her address
on a piece of paper you just happened to have spare,
and arrange to definitely see her
sometime, somewhere.

And then, on the market side of that walkway was the upstairs of Mace's pet shop where I drooled for hours on end, nose pressed breathily close to the thick, warm glass of giant fish tanks, ogling tiny, transparent Angel Fish - how did anyone make fish that were see-through? - drifting aimlessly, back and forth, with bubbly lengths of tubing attached to the backs of their strange, underwater, jungle-like plant world. I'd bring some back home on the bus with me, in squashy polythene bags, hoping and praying that they wouldn't leak all over my trousers. They often didn't. And they lived long enough so that you didn't have to go back and buy more for at least a couple of weeks - or so.

I just couldn't stop looking when I saw that
you could see through angel fish,
and that they were such a lovely colour.
I had to do a bit of sacrificing though
to get them and all the clobber you needed:
three hamsters and one white mouse sold,
and no more Christmases and birthdays for me
until 2020.

That street was our playground. When my Uncle Kenneth bought a grey, second-hand Morris Minor in 1967, it was one of the very first cars to be parked out in that street. Coningsby Road, by and large, was the property of children in those days. It was where races were run, and new-cum-old bikes put through their paces. It was where children took it in turns to swing round and round the gas lamp post until dizziness set in. My first second-hand bicycle - I remember accidentally seeing my grandfather giving it a spanking new coat of red paint out in the back yard - was a Christmas gift. I was five years old. By the afternoon of Boxing Day I was out in the street, pedal-wobbling along, steadied only by my uncle's hand on the saddle as he came running along behind. Were there odder people roaming the streets of Fir Vale in those years or does the vulnerability of childhood exaggerate one's fears and apprehensions? The tramps' ward that backed onto Herries Road had its fair share of oddities. There was the alarming, wild-eyed old man who wore several overcoats and two or three hats all at once in all weathers. He used to come down Herries Road, talking to himself in a very loud voice, and making wild, swinging gestures in the direction of phantom enemies. Then, one Sunday morning when Uncle Ken and I were lovingly cleaning the chrome of the bumper of his Morris Minor with Duraglit, a man appeared with his wife from around Fir Vale Road way, pushing a juddery old pram. He started to talk to Uncle Ken, very quickly, very urgently, but nothing that he said seemed to make any sense. He didn't have any roof to his mouth, I discovered later. As he spoke into the face of my uncle, he was jabbing in the direction of the pram, over and over. His wife's red, head-scarved face seemed to be hooked over his shoulder as he talked. Did we want to buy a second-hand radio by any chance? he was asking as he pointed into the pram. No thanks, mester, not today.

Harold

It is not easy to write about my grandfather. I knew him well, and yet I did not know him at all. In character, he was rigid and disciplinarian. He walked with a stick, flinging it out in front of him as if he were still marching in a military parade. Every day he took the same short walk 'round the lump' as he put it, which meant walking up Herries Road, back along Crabtree Close, and down Barnsley Road until he met the other end of our road again. The routine was as regular and as dependable in its trajectory as the slow, circular crawl of the minute hand around the perimeter of our kitchen clock.

He did not encourage intimacy. Is that wholly unsurprising though, given that he was one of the few men from the Sheffield Battalion to have survived the horrors of the Somme? His demeanour was quite different from that of my grandmother Mabel. Harold was always to be seen standing or sitting bolt upright, facing indomitably into the future. He dressed smartly on almost all occasions, often in a sports jacket, with the tongue of a folded white handkerchief lolling out of his breast pocket. He was immensely proud of his appearance. In the days before we took our annual holiday, usually by hot, heaving coach, to Blackpool, I would see him in front of the kitchen mirror, carefully applying Grecian 2000 to his abundant flourish of grey hair, which was always swept straight back from his forehead as if by a mighty wind, with an old toothbrush. He was always loud and assertive. In his opinion, his was the voice to be listened to. He made his presence felt at all times. He expected things to be done at very particular moments, and woe betide if there was any disturbance of the usual arrangements. He became ever more demanding as he aged and declined into dependency, turning my mother into a profoundly unwilling slave to his every beck and call during his final years of sad decrepitude. He was self-sufficient and self-propelling to an almost alarming extent until then. He would repair his own clothes when occasion demanded. Many is the time I have seen him sitting behind the old black Singer Sewing Machine at the kitchen table, sucking at the end of the thread which he would shortly be inserting into the torpedo-shaped metal shuttle. Trousers and shirts would require attention, constantly. As his waist grew, so his trousers demanded the rapid insertion of gussets into the rear - v-shaped pieces of cloth to give his behind and his waistline more capacity to expand. He would expect meal times to be at very particular moments of day, and at always the same time. 'Are we having a bit of something then, Doff?' he would ask of my mother, sternly glancing up at the clock as the hour hand crept towards nine. It was inconceivable that we would ever begin to eat supper - a light meal of a cup

53

of tea and bread and cheddar cheese and a pickled onion or two most often - after nine o'clock. Once in bed, he would want to know when my mother too would be retiring. 'Are you coming up then, Doff?' he'd shout. He did not like the idea of her sitting, idly reading, as he lay awake in his bed in the front bedroom. During my childhood, the small and hectic world of 45 Coningsby Road danced to the tune of Harold Hickson.

My grandmother Mabel, by comparison, was small, rotund, meek and patiently suffering. My grandfather's voice still rings loud in my ears when I choose to swivel my head in his direction. It is as if I am standing on the parade ground, arms held stiffly to my sides. My grandmother I can scarcely hear at all, though I do still vividly see her there, in the corner of that tiny kitchen at Coningsby Road. She is bent far over, knees unflexed, sweeping the carpet with a hand brush, uncomplaining, patient and machine-like in her docility. That was how she always was, toiling for others: cooking, washing clothes at the sink, consoling those who needed consolation, always small and bent forward. In photographs she seldom smiles or looks animated. Weary resignation – that is the pose she usually strikes in the photographs that I have of her. Although she often wore good clothes out of doors, she seemed to take no real pride in her appearance. She had given up the ghost with her appearance. By contrast, my grandfather took immense pride in his. He was accountable to the world. She was accountable to nothing more extensive than the kitchen floor.

Our return to Coningsby Road after the failure of my mother's first marriage was not easy. My grandmother was infinitely kindly and accommodating, my grandfather much less so. Yes, the Second World War and the way it had transformed my father during those long years of absence in the Far East, had an unpredictable impact upon Harold's life. He had not expected us to be living with him in that small terraced house in Sheffield at all. He had not expected my mother to arrive there, pregnant, with suitcase in hand and a small daughter, at the bitter end of that terrible winter of 1948.

This is how my mother told it. When my father returned from Burma in 1945, my mother barely recognised him. She explained all this to me years later, when she was an old woman. War destroyed many human relationships - and I am not referring to the tragic deaths of combatants. I mean that during enforced separations of several years, the best intentioned of human beings can grow apart from each other. And so it was with my mother and my father. The man who arrived back at Coningsby Road one day from Burma, unannounced, was quite different in colour and character from the man who had left. His skin had been tanned almost black by the Asian sun. He wore long mustaches, twisted to points and flamboyantly waxed. She fainted when she saw him. He asked her to go on holiday with him. She refused. She did not want to be separated from her daughter, she said. The relationship was uneasy. He worked as a nurse at the local hospital. When he worked nights, he would refuse to take a house key with him - which meant that when he returned late at night from his shift at the hospital, he would wake everyone in the house up by bagging on the door to be admitted. In short, he was not happy at 45 Coningsby Road. When he came home in the evenings, he would lie down on the sofa in the kitchen and cover his face with a blanket. There he would lie, unbudging, unspeaking, for hours at a time.

Eventually she agreed to return to live in Manchester, his native town. They took a rented house in Stretford. He worked in a local hospital. Sometimes he would not return at nights. She was left on her own, looking after a small child. She became pregnant with a second. According to my mother, he refused to believe that it was his. One day she picked up a suitcase and, small child in hand, took the train back to her parents' house in Sheffield. That foetus was me.

My grandparents had agreed to have her back, but the house was scarcely big enough for us all. My childhood is full of memories of ferocious arguments between my mother and my grandfather. Money - or rather the lack of it - was usually at the root of these disputes.

On Friday nights, the rattly old black tin would come out. My grandfather would open it with a small key. Inside there would be money - bills and small change - and scribbled notes. My mother and my grandmother would be questioned about that week's housekeeping, how and on what exactly it had been spent. Voices would be raised, bits of scribbled-on paper flourished in the air. The air itself would turn blue. I heard what I took to be the word 'blood' used, repeatedly. The room seemed to be full of this word. I joined in: 'blood, blood, blood' I shouted at the top of my small voice.

Dorothy

My mother could have made a powerful impression upon the world. She failed to do so. She was a woman of independent spirit and outspokenness, rancorous, pugnacious, ever ready to express her opinions. She was also utterly timid, afraid of the world and of other people. She was forever wittlin and mitherin. She had almost no friends. She had a loathing of social occasions. She cleaved to her family, and to no one else. The rest of the world was wholly untrustworthy and utterly alien. She welcomed no species of foreignness, whether it be of the human kind or a mouthful of spaghetti. She trusted only what she knew, and she knew very little. And yet she was not without talent. She played the piano beautifully and with great flamboyance, but no public ever heard her play. She gave performances only for her immediate family. She drew with talent as a schoolgirl - she could easily have flourished at an art college - but no such opportunities were open to her, and consequently I have no memories of seeing her draw.

Hers was a thwarted life. And yet who was to blame for this? Blame the times if you like - there were few opportunities for a woman like Dorothy when she was growing up. She worked intermittently, in a milk bar in Fargate during the 1950s, and as a cleaner when I was a small boy - I remember wandering around houses she was cleaning - she would take me with her - opening cupboards, or sitting on alien chairs in houses smarter than ours, kicking my feet and day-dreaming. Many years later, when my sister and I were grown up, we would have arguments with her about her lack of ambition, her inability to make something of her life. She would round on us ferociously for criticising her. Nothing ever changed. She remained locked inside that small house, defeated by circumstances, under the thumb of her father, who ruled that household with a rod of iron. Was she ever truly happy at Coningsby Road? Yes, I remember some of her fleeting moments of happiness. Late at night, after everyone else had gone to bed, she would take out her library book - probably a Jean Plaidy or a Georgette Heyer - and the slender green pack of five Woodbines and smoke, one cigarette after another, and read for an hour. She was alone with herself then, away from the call of my grandfather's voice, at peace for a change, in a tranquil house.

Did I ever talk much to her about the things that really concerned me? The answer, sadly, is no. We lived alongside each other, life-long. I cared for her, I felt a need to protect her from pain. I suffered pain and anxiety when she was in pain. I also felt utterly helpless at such times. But for much of my life, as child and adult, I felt utterly remote from her, as if I was inhabiting a private kingdom. I knew that I wanted it to be like that. I wanted there to be that breathing space between us so that I could think and dream entirely separately from her. It gave me a great sense of inner freedom to do so. Her views on politics were simple, brutish, tribal. She read her books of historical fiction from Firth Park Library with a passionate commitment, but she would not have wanted to enter into a conversation about books in general or literature in the abstract. She never read any of the books that I read. She might pick one up and tut-tut, and shake her head. All she did was to admire me, at a distance, for liking them - which was generous of her. We almost never talked about poetry. I remember just two occasions. One evening – I must have been about sixteen years old when this happened - I was sitting next to her beside a roaring fire in the kitchen. Everyone else must have gone to bed. A few days before, I had found an anthology of poems, a small blue book with very thin paper, thin enough to belong to a Bible. My mother knew that book. She told me that it contained the only poem that she really loved. This was a long narrative poem by Arthur Noyes called 'The Highwayman'. She could remember the chorus and parts of the poem too. She recited whole chunks of it out loud to me, with some excitement in her voice. She loved the romantic figure of the highwayman himself – 'he'd a French cocked hat on his forehead, and a bunch of lace at his chin...' – and his strange trysts at the inn. She loved the fact that he'd come galloping along a lonely highway, illumined by 'a ribbon of moonlight'. She loved the poem's compulsive, surging, jog-trot rhythms. Much later in her life she recited parts of Wordsworth's 'The Daffodils' to me, from memory. She had remembered it from her school days.

Going to the local cinema was one of her greatest pleasures. She would make the visit twice a week, usually on her own, on Mondays and Thursdays, because that is when the programme would change. Later we would go together, to see *Spartacus, Ben Hur, King of Kings,* all extraordinary spectacles with casts of thousands, roaring, cheering or on the murderous rampage. I would marvel, boggle-eyed, at the rippling muscles of Charlton Heston, projected onto a screen of such awe-inspiring size and presence. And then on Saturday mornings, my sister Pat and I would queue up for the children's matinee and the pleasures of Charlie Chaplin, Buster Keaton, the Three Stooges and the heroics of Captain Marvel, who always said: Shazam! And did we not all, cheering, say it after him? What in the outside world could ever measure up to this?

There had been so many flourishing cinemas in Sheffield in the years before I was born. Even as a boy, I was within walking distance of at least six of them. They had names which still resonate: the Roxy, the Forum, the Colisseum, the Gaumont. Their names were fanciful evocations of the vanished glories of the Roman Empire. Others were boarded up, abandoned, unloved beside the road. These cinemas were not the small and meagre multiple-plexes of the present, engineered to suit niche audiences of such and such a size. They were grandiose palaces of pleasure, worlds created to be luxuriously fantastical alternatives to the realities of the street outside. Such a palace was the Sunbeam in Fir Vale. How could such a small Sheffield suburb as Fir Vale have possessed such a place? It stood within a quarter of a mile of our house. You ran out of the front door, down Blyde Road to the Bottom. From there you could see it, set back, the largest building in Fir Vale by a mile.

The Sunbeam Cinema in Fir Vale was an ever self-renewing place of delights to us. It felt so mysteriously huge and so darkly opulent, with its curving rows of red velvet seats, its eerily back-lit statuettes in niches, all a little faded and beaten down by the time of our regular visits. Between the features - there would always be two films in those days, an A and a B together with the Pathé News, whose arrival would be heralded by the crowing of an enormous cock - usherettes would come hurrying to the front of the house, carrying large, illuminated trays bearing ice cream in tubs, which would be eaten with the aid of small, spade-like spoons concealed just beneath the cardboard lid.

And then, one day, it was boarded up, and soon demolished. By then the era of television was upon us, and audiences had diminished to a trickle, which made that vast interior seem even more ghostly and woe-begone. I remember, late one morning, standing there in front it as the wreckers were doing their worst. I remember the great metal ball, attached to the end of a chain, swinging at the top-most part of the wall of the facade, and of parts of it falling, just a few yards in front of me, in a pother of brick dust. When it was all over, I visited the sad, empty site at the bottom of Barnsley Road. A petrol station would soon rise up there. I marvelled at how small a space the Sunbeam had occupied. Could it really be true? Could so much really have been contained within so small a space? Inside, the space had always seemed so huge, with its tiers of red velvet seats, and the way the curtains opened to reveal the screen...

Dorothy had been born in 1916, the very year that her father – my grandfather Harold - went to the Somme with the Sheffield Battalion. It is almost impossible to imagine how terrible it must have been for my grandmother Mabel, left helplessly and hopelessly alone, all that tension of fearing and waiting, with her new born child in Fir Vale, as her husband waged war. We can take a kind of perverse, fragmentary comfort of sorts in the knowledge that there was such censorship of the truth in those days. The appalling losses and tactical blunders were not immediately apparent to the suffering families back home. We now know that the government would allow only a maximum of two corpses to be photographed together at any one time. Such was the strict censorship in those years before technology removed the power of governments to keep their people in the dark about their tragic and disgraceful misdemeanours.

My grandfather said nothing about his own experience of the horrors of this war within our earshot. As far as I am aware there were just two people to whom he ever confided the truth, his own wife Mabel and the Sheffield novelist John Harris, who incorporated the information that Harold gave him into a fictional account of the conflict called *Covenant with Death*. This book sat high on the wall, wedged amongst a handful of others – this was the extent of our library at Coningsby Road - in our small kitchen bookcase, carefully protected by anonymous-looking brown parcel paper, throughout most of my young life there. It was not until two years before her own death, in 2007, that my mother Dorothy confided to me what Harold had told Mabel about the wholesale, near total destruction of the Sheffield Battalion at the Somme. Here is an edited transcription of that conversation from the summer of 2007, which took place in the living room of her council house in Totley, overlooking her beloved garden with its rows of geraniums in full bloom, one warm Saturday afternoon as she gently sucked on a Fox's Glacier Mint rather in the way that Harold himself would have done. By then my mother was 91 years of age. She would die two years and three months later in the Northern General Hospital.

Michael: How did he find out that so many of his friends had died?

Dorothy: When they did the roll call at the end of the day, only ten men of the six hundred who went over the top reported. Harold was amongst that ten. He told my mother that when he came home.

Michael: He himself must have seen them die then…

Dorothy: The runner directly in front of him was blown up, shot to pieces. He could hear the wailing of all his mates who had been caught up on the barbed wire. There was nothing they could do for them. Nobody dared help them. All that wailing and screaming and shouting for help went on all through the day and all through the night. It was terrible, that noise, all that moaning and crying. They just had to leave them to die.

Michael: The German trenches were very close by, of course…

Dorothy: The trenches were only a few yards apart. The Germans had tunnels underneath the allied trenches. They could hear them banging about…

Michael: Do you know how many of Harold's close friends survived?

Dorothy: He was the only one to survive of all his close mates in Fir Vale. They were all killed. Harold sent letters to my mother to tell her. He became a kind of messenger boy for all the others. The wives used to come to my mother to get the news. None of the others wrote of course because they were either wounded or killed. My mother used to dread his letters coming because it was always bad news. There was only ever bad news.

One thing alone stirred Dorothy herself into action. When Coningsby Road was threatened with demolition in the second half of the 1970s, she fought with fervour and aplomb to save it. She failed to do so, but she was offered a council house in Totley, one of the most desirable districts of Sheffield, to appease her spirited nature. Otherwise, she lived a rather loveless life during the years that I lived with her. She was attracted to men, but she allowed no man to court her after the failure of her first marriage - until an enterprising carpet layer from Liverpool called Wilfred Welsby came on the scene in the second half of the 1970s. As a result of this liaison a tiny whiff of scandal hung in the air - Wilf deserted his first wife for Dorothy. I have always felt that this did not entirely displease her.

A common language bonds us. The way a language is spoken also sets us apart from each other. I no longer sound much like the boy who grew up in the north-east of Sheffield. I both slightly regret that fact and accept that it is inevitable. When we move from place to place, we adapt to our new surroundings. We come to sound like those amongst whom we mingle. We need to belong somewhere. Dorothy lived almost nowhere but Sheffield. She made just one brief foray outside United Kingdom, and that was to Paris, where I took her in the 1980s. I remember to this day her dread at seeing the foodstuffs on offer in a Vietnamese restaurant, all those alien lumps of this and that, afloat in semi-opaque, foreign waters. It would not have entirely surprised her if a miniature shark had reared its head out of that the soup bowl. She was threading her fearful way, with bated breath, through a country of the strange. Yes, almost everywhere was Other to Dorothy, to be feared and shunned with palpable looks of horror and disgust – there was no refinement to Dorothy's rejections, no hints of gratitude. She made her feelings obvious, immediately, and at all times.

And yet her attitude towards the language as she heard it spoken around her was odd and strangely complicated. She disliked what she described as broad, rough or common talk. She used words of Sheffield dialect, but she was not exactly proud of doing so. When she did so, it was as if she was on a stage, playing up to an audience. The fact is that she was who was, and she could not help herself. Her children were quite another matter. She wanted them to better themselves socially and linguistically. She believed that there were better ways of speaking than the way she spoke, even though she did her best to sound as respectable and as little like some of the near neighbours as possible. She sent my sister to elocution lessons at a house along Page Hall Road to knock the rougher Sheffield edges off her speech. And yet she was quick to despise anyone whom she thought was la-di-da, which meant pretending to get above themselves socially by putting on a posh voice, and behaving in such a way as to suggest that they were something other than the person they had been born. My sister loathed these elocution lessons. She quickly settled back into being herself. You are tethered to the place of your birth by a ball and chain.

I was my mother's beloved son, her most favoured object. I could do no wrong. This both pleased me and disgusted me in just about equal measure. At times I felt so stifled by her affections that I wanted to shrug her off altogether. I did not do so because I was not quite capable of such baseness, such cruelty. My sister suffered because I was the favoured one. She and my mother fought lifelong. There was nothing to be done to stop it. Eventually my mother died, and my sister was released. That is how I feel driven to express it.

Sometimes my mother treated my sister with genuine malignity. I feel ashamed to this day even to recall it. I still own the photograph of my sister's wedding day in 1963, almost fifty years ago. Bride and groom are standing outside St Cuthbert's Anglican Church in full sunlight, hand in hand. The door of the black wedding car hangs open, expectantly. I can see Fir Vale and its row of shops at the bottom of the hill behind them. Those are the shops that I remember so well, all long gone. In particular, there was Gabbitas, my particular favourite, which sold the *Dandy* and the *Beano* and sherbet to be sucked into the mouth with the aid of black licorice pipes, and those small paper bags full of chocolate-coated toffees. Bride and groom look stunningly beautiful, blessed by good fortune, in the prime of their young lives, as they stand there in the sunshine.

My sister Pat was just twenty-one years of age when she married for the first time. If my mother had had her way, this marriage might well not have happened at all. My mother treated my sister's husband-to-be with contempt. He came from the wrong part of Sheffield, the east end, Attercliffe. He was socially beneath her. It is scarcely to be credited that a woman from one poor, working-class district of Sheffield could have looked down upon a young man who came from another such area - and yet that is the sad truth of the matter. Haydn, in Dorothy's opinion, deserved to be looked down upon. In fact, he was a stunning young man. I first met him when I was perhaps twelve year old. He took Elvis Presley as his role model. He would spend long, long minutes perfecting his long, glossy, barrel-shaped black quiff in front of the mirror in our kitchen. I would watch him, awe-struck. When I shook his hand for the first time, I discovered that he had the most powerful grip I had ever come across. His fingers felt long, oily and unusually supple. These things too took me aback. He was also intensely fashion-conscious. For a man who had seemingly emerged from poverty and social disadvantage, he seemed to be surprisingly well - if not impeccably - dressed: sharp blue suit, black winkle pickers, and, of course, that extraordinarily elegant quiff. Haydn had a very particular way of wielding a comb, leaning back slightly, knees slightly flexed, as he stroked it through his gleaming black hair that he watched so attentively in the kitchen mirror above the fireplace. And then there was the additional problem of quite where and how to position his cap in order not in any way to disturb the gently forward-diving swoop of that sculpted quiff. I was astonished by the long minutes that this mirror ritual could go on for. There was no swift and easy road to physical perfection. If this was vanity, it deserved serious study. As I watched all this happen - and it seemed to happen with great regularity - I would wonder to myself, even then as a young teenager, how all this could be reconciled with everything that my mother told me about the wretchedness of Attercliffe, those rows of black terraced housing huddled in the shadows of the steel mills. I knew very little of the place myself. Why should one?

As I see myself sitting there in a chair beside the table in the kitchen of 45 Coningsby Road swinging my legs almost fifty years ago, I find that I am looking at not one but several profiles. There is Haydn, my sometime future brother-in-law, side on to the mirror, attending to his quiff, but I can also see - this time with the benefit of hindsight - the image of the face of that truck driver's son from Tennessee who took the world of popular music by storm in the second half of the 1950s. Yes, I can so easily recognise the face of Elvis Presley in that look on Haydn's face, that extraordinary leer of his, and as I look at Elvis through the face of Haydn, I can also see other images superimposed upon Haydn's, the images of Haydn's two sons, Richard and James, both now handsome grown men. They too have that same Elvis leer. It has been passed down from generation to generation. Elvis may have faded somewhat - just as the smile of the Cheshire Cat faded as Alice stared at it - but he is certainly not dead.

Other aspects of Haydn fascinated me too. He had a most dreadful, near disabling, stammer. In fact, at times he seemed barely able to spit out his words at all. I felt shocked and saddened by this. What is more, this handicap made me feel somewhat at one with him. I too had verbal and visual tics from early childhood on. One day I would find it impossible to stop myself opening my mouth as widely as possible, for example, over and over again, as if life were almost entirely about the compulsive need to open your mouth as far as it would go - or, at the very least, to test your ability to do so over and over again. I was in the grip of something that I seemed incapable of controlling. My mother said nothing to me about any of this. She simply failed to acknowledge that anything was happening at all. Perhaps she would have found it uncomfortable to acknowledge that I was less than perfect in various respects. When I travelled on a tram on my own as a child - the tram, for example, that would carry me from Firs Hill Primary School down the hill as far as Fir Vale - no more than half a mile's distance - I would find myself growing terribly anxious as I waited for the tram to arrive. I knew how difficult it would be for me to say the words that I needed to say to the conductor: 'P-penny one, please.' There is nothing worse than a plosive for a stammerer, and I was for quite some time one of those - until some other embarrassing tic seized hold of me.

And almost everything that would ever happen to me in those days of my young life seemed to happen in this house. My universe pivoted about it. There was little additional travelling - except for that wonderful annual trip to Mrs Ansells' boarding house in Blackpool.

Blackpool

Mrs Ansell's boarding house was a little bit like our own house, but bigger and posher. It was in a terraced street, but this one was not across the road from a tramps' ward. It huddled in the lee of the mighty Imperial Hotel, which itself faced the chill of the Irish Sea, at the north end of the town. Its big bay window, against which the table was set for a sunny breakfast – the sun always seemed to come in through that window at breakfast time - allowed us a good view of families rushing past with their beach balls and towels. We would sit outside on the bench in Mrs Ansell's tiny front garden, soaking it all up, smelling the breeze from off the sea, watching the seagulls wheeling and swooping as they shrieked at us for titbits. My memories of that place are both good and painful. I remember my mother's regular constipation, and how it went on for days and days, all the miserable, behind-the-hands talk about the smallness and the hardness of her stools, and how I pitied her when she looked at me, always so woebegone. I so often pitied and felt for my mother when she was in pain, and she was, it seems, so often in one kind of physical pain or another. There would be the regular throbbing head aches, for example, and the neat white boxes of white aspirin to cure it. And then there was the sciatica in her leg, which we both felt helpless to cure or the weekly visits to Dr Walsh's surgery at the top of Owler Lane. How many hours I must have spent sitting in that crowded waiting room with all those other poor souls, leafing idly through dog-eared copies of last season's magazines. My mother liked Dr Walsh. He was stout and Irish and jovially talkative, with a watch chain that looped across his stomach, and he possessed more than a touch of saucy Irish banter. I used to dread the sight of the needle he would bring out to inject into my mother's upper leg for her anaemia. It was so fearsomely long and thick.

It was quite a rigmarole, unbuttoning the pink button of her pink garter belt to release the top of her stocking. I felt she quite liked fussing over that bit of the procedure as Dr Walsh stood there, needle brimming with colourless serum raised skyward, laughing and joking with her. I too had anaemia, according to my mother, until I was about fifteen years old. Why else was I always so terribly pale? She had red iron tablets prescribed for me, and I popped them in dutifully every day of my life until one late afternoon, on a visit to my Uncle Norman's house near Bedford, my brusque Aunt Esmé, who, according to my mother, thought she had bettered herself by leaving Sheffield, told my mother that my so called anaemia was so much nonsense, and threw the entire box of tablets into her bin. I never took them after that. My mother never mentioned my anaemia again. And life went on for me much as it had before.

No, Mrs Ansell's food just did not agree with my mother. The truth is that no one's food agreed with my mother except the simple, predictable kind that was cooked in her own kitchen. Well, there was one exception: the hot, well battered lengths of haddock, accompanied by steaming chips doused in salt and malt vinegar, and then wrapped in newspaper, from one of the many fish bars along the Promenade. My mother seemed to have no problems at all with fish and chips.

But to more than offset all that deep-bowel misery, there was the wonder of the hundreds of slot machines at the Olympia, the excitement of staring in at all those little metal cranes behind glass as they nearly picked up a toy from an enormous heap of wonderful gifts, and nearly – but in fact almost never - dropped it down the chute in exchange for my pennies. Yes, it almost never came to pass, but I always believed that the next time it would. The marvel was that unlike on other weeks of the year, there were always, in the one-week wonderland of Blackpool, yet more pennies and sixpences and shillings to be doled out to me from the purse in the handbag that swung from my mother's arm. That precious holiday week was such a time between times, such a casting off of worry and adversity of (almost) every kind. In the evenings, there would be shows to go to, and every night we strolled through the big swinging doors of this theatre or that theatre as if we were rolling in the stuff, flourishing our tickets at the doorman. Once inside, we sat back to watch big girls in feathery little hats link arms and kick out their beefy legs or comedians in silly hats falling all over the stage, pretending to be drunk. Even my mother might have agreed that there was nothing funnier than a man pretending to be drunk in a Blackpool theatre. And, during the day, blustery Lancastrian weather permitting, there would be much idling along the north end of the beach – quieter and more respectable than the south end, said my mother - with my sister, who would be sunbathing in her one-piece with her friend Milly in glasses, as I hid beneath a towel, squirming deep into the sand. I always hated the sun on my skin. Meanwhile, Harold and Mabel would be seated just a short distance away, on one of those long green benches along the promenade, staring seaward. Harold's arm would be propped on the knob end of his stick. Mabel would be sitting, utterly impassive, neither enjoying herself nor not enjoying herself, I always felt, wearing one of her straw hats, hands folded one over the other, taking it all in. Just occasionally I would creep up behind her with my mother's camera and photograph that hat from above, recording its gentle turns.

This annual coach trip to Blackpool was one of the few great and regular moments of family celebration (another was Christmas), times set apart from the rest on account of their specialness. On these occasions, that abiding watchfulness about money was thrown to the winds. It was as if at these two points in the awful, penny-pinching grind of the year, so carefully separated from each other by six-monthly intervals, the usual rules and prohibitions were tossed to the four winds. New clothes were purchased in which to flaunt ourselves along the sea front. Once in that magical holiday terrain, gifts were purchased with near reckless abandon. I remember so well not only that I was once allowed to buy three gifts for myself when at the seaside - one of these was a sailing boat which would later become the pride of the Firth Park Boating Pond - but that we would eat out at a fish and chip shop almost every night of the week, carrying the whiff of hot, lightly salted and heavily vinegared chips for as long as they would last in the general direction of the Pleasure Beach and, legs and weather permitting, even beyond.

I last visited Blackpool at the age of seventeen. By then I was spending most of my time sitting apart from my relatives, scribbling poem after poem in spiral-bound notebooks, and reading the books that I had brought with me. By then, I had a reading agenda in my head, and consequently I would always be carrying my books with me. I can see myself sitting on that bench outside Mrs Ansell's bay window, reading *Modern Man In Search of a Soul* by C.J. Jung, and quietly ignoring the happy beachcombers that were passing by with their beach balls, their kites, and their plastic bats to which rubber balls were attached by long lengths of elastic. The superior life of the mind had evidently begun.

To an extent, it must seem a saddening admission that I was the victim of such confinement for so long, that there were so few visitors to that house in Coningsby Road, and that most of the absentees should have included the great majority of our relatives. In fact, it scarcely saddened me at all that my mother lacked the knack of sociability, that she chose to shun others, and to neglect her few friends. A child compensates. If castles of brick are not to be built, one builds castles of air. And so it was with me. I made much of seemingly little. Even though the household possessed few books - there was a single small book case in the kitchen which, like the wireless which faced it from the opposite side of the room, was positioned high up on the wall, and was no more than about one foot wide - there were enough of them to quicken an appetite. I remember a dictionary, Harold's well thumbed copy of *A Tale of Two Cities* - he read this book every year - and that mysterious volume to which I have already referred called *A Covenant*

With Death, which was protected by brown parcel paper.

Needless to say, in later life I have amply compensated for this relatively bookless childhood.

The terror of war recedes:
Mabel with Dorothy, c. 1918

Taking it easy at Crimicar Lane in the 1940s:
(l. to r.) Harold, Mabel, family friend Kitty, Pat, Dorothy

The father Michael never knew:
Sid with his daughter Pat in the 1940s

Robert Mitchum's biggest fan:
Dorothy with her damaged tooth in the 1950s

Under mother's thumb: the young
school boy with the grip in his hair

'An outside lavvy's not a bad thing though, Especially when the greens make you feel sick...'

Road to freedom: the cobbled gennel leading out of our back yard

'The only Sunbeam lighting up Fir Vale...'

The man with the perfect quiff from Attercliffe: my sister Pat with her new husband Haydn on her wedding day, Fir Vale, 1963

Carefree Strollers:
Michael, Dorothy and Pat at the seaside, c.1956

Seaside swelter: outside Mrs Ansell's boarding house in Blackpool in the 1960s, (l. to r.) Harold, Michael, unknown, Mabel, unknown, Dorothy

Aerial view:
Mabel and Harold on the Promenade, Blackpool

Breezy Spot: Dorothy and
Mabel beside the sea

Blue rinses for the ladies:
Olive Fields the Hairdresser at Fir Vale
Bottom in the 1970s

Soon to be swept away: Coningsby
Road at the end of the 1970s

Father in all but name:
Uncle Ken cossets a new-born

Michael Glover, editor of
Target Books, shares a joke
with Jon Pertwee, the third
incarnation of Doctor Who,
in 1974

Kenneth

Every boy needs a father. And especially a boy who does not have a father. I heard almost nothing of my father during the nineteen years that I lived at 45 Coningsby Road. There was talk of unpaid alimony, of visits by my mother to the Sheffield Courthouse, and of fleeting, acrimonious encounters. I was said to have been present in the same courtroom as Sid Glover on at least one occasion. According to my mother, he didn't look at me. Unacknowledged for a second time then. In fact, all this scarcely mattered to me because the truth is that I did not miss him at all. How could I miss a man I had not even met? Why would I need yet another person when that tiny, hot, bright kitchen was already full to bursting with people?

There was someone else though. I had my own substitute father in the person of my mother's brother, Uncle Kenneth. It was he who became my father in all but name, he with whom I forged a special bond.

Uncle Ken was - and remains as I write these words - a rare spirit. He was a tall, gentle, unemphatic man. He understood the values of circumspection and silence. He taught me the art of not speaking. I could tell when he was both present in a room and absent from it in all but body. I could tell when he was inhabiting and exploring worlds of his own private imaginings. He helped me to value taciturnity, unsociability. He was an unflamboyant man. This too intrigued me. He was evidently in hiding from the world of the everyday. There was a lot to be known which would not be easily discovered. As with any person who says very little, who looks but seldom speaks, I believed him to be boundlessly clever. What a role model for an aspiring writer!

In the end he became an accountant by profession, but in his heart of hearts he had wanted, at a certain point in his life, to be a novelist. He even wrote a novel - it was called *The Double Corner* - for which he failed to find a publisher. He later destroyed it. I regretted that act, but I also regarded it as heroic. He valued literature, and he read a great deal. We still regularly discuss the books that he is reading. What is more, he valued committing his thoughts, his imaginings, to paper. He used to keep a small, red notebook - I would occasionally catch sight of it on the edge of the kitchen table - in which he would write, in pencil, in a small hand, and the sight of that notebook helped to quicken my own literary ambitions. Its very presence there said to me, *sotto voce*: there are extraordinary worlds beyond the confining world of this small kitchen. You do not have to travel far physically to find them.

There were mysteries surrounding my uncle and his writing and his

reading. As a teenager, I used to read what he read in public after him —
the weekly *Observer* on a Sunday, and also *Encounter* magazine, to which he
subscribed, and which used to plop onto the door mat once a month, in a
large, stiff, brown envelope. I loved *Encounter*. I loved how dense and thick
and serious it always looked. It was part-edited by a poet in those days —
Stephen Spender — and it began to open out to me an entire world in which
literature intermeshed in strange and interesting ways with global politics.
But I was mystified by my uncle's writing too. He never showed it to me —
why should he? But, more to the point, I never saw him writing more than
the merest fragment of a note or two in that notebook of his, in pencil, at
the kitchen table. He would never say anything before he wrote something
down. And, having done so, usually quite quickly, he would never comment
upon the fact that he had just committed a thought to paper. Nor would
we. It would have been an intrusion, we all instinctively felt. It was as if
his hand had been acting on its own, for the sake of exercise alone, almost
without his knowledge. His facial expressions never changed either. He still
looked as blandly kind and mild-mannered as ever. But what exactly had
he written in that book just then? Had he written something about us or
had his thoughts transported him to China, where Chairman Mao and his
equally mysterious Red Guards were on the loose? Was he perhaps plotting
against us or laughing at us? Surely not. We loved him too much for that.
No, he loved us too much for that. How could I ever be sure though?
Where in the world were his thoughts at that moment? I would look at him
across the kitchen table, and he would wink back at me fondly, inclining his
head slightly as he did so.

But if he was a writer, where was he mainly doing his writing? Not in this
house, that was for sure. At some point I discovered, quite by chance, that
he was renting a room somewhere, but I never knew where, and I was never
invited to go there. (I later discovered that this place was the rehearsal room
of the theatre group to which he belonged. It was in the centre of the city,
tucked away somewhere behind the Hippodrome.) What is more, he didn't
look like a writer, and he seldom talked about being a writer. Which means
that he didn't play at being a writer. Some writers I had already heard of
and read about were noisy, boozy rebels, living on the edge of dangerous
worlds of serious non-conformity. My uncle was never like that. He never
looked like a hell-raising non-conformist. He always wore a sober suit and
a tie. Greys. Restrained greens. Those were my uncle's colours of choice.
Perhaps that was a little disappointing to me. And yet it also made the fact
of him being amongst us even more interesting, as if he was cunningly
outwitting the usual stereotype of the writer by pretending to be the most

ordinary of people. And yet there always remained strange, niggling, unanswered questions I wanted to put to him, had I ever felt it was right to do so. I seldom did – except once. I knew that he loved the works of D.H. Lawrence. I also knew that Lawrence had been a rebel – *Lady Chatterley's Lover*, that book that I later found, half in bits in the tall boy of our front bedroom, was prosecuted for indecency when I was fourteen years old - and that he had written with openness and fervour about sexuality. What did my uncle think about Lawrence and the issue of sex? I could never tell. He would always seem to be hanging back inside himself, not wanting, I felt, to reveal his hand to me.

My relationship with my uncle was both simple and complicated. He cared for me in a way that no other man did. For years we had our weekly rituals. As a boy he would take me to Longley Park every Sunday afternoon to play football. We would walk together up Herries Road, which bounds the sprawl of the Northern General Hospital. At the top end of the hospital's grounds there used to be a farm – yet another of those examples of surviving remnants of nature within reach of Fir Vale. We would feed grass to a chestnut foal which would come walking towards the wall when it saw us strolling by. On Wednesday nights he would take me to the Cartoon Cinema in Fitzalan Square for my weekly dose of Tom and Jerry, Pluto and Speedy Gonzales. On Saturday afternoon, we would go to Bramall Lane and pay one shilling and sixpence to watch Sheffield United and its team of doughty, modestly paid local players - Cec Coldwell at the back, Joe Shaw in the centre of defence, Alan Hodgkinson in goal, Alan Simpson streaking down the left wing. Week after week - on alternate weeks we would often watch the reserve team - I would stand beside my uncle on the open terracing in my red and white scarf, cheering and wildly rotating my rackety wooden rattle as the rain siled down at just the right angle to trickle down your neck. Then, as now, United were not the best of teams. They were the city's underdogs, and we loved them for that. They never had as many supporters as Sheffield Wednesday. Success was always just about to happen. Meanwhile, they fought on, doggedly, usually in the second division of the old league, neither close to the top nor close to the bottom. They played a kind of rough, valiant football, without too much finesse, punting the ball vast distances, running like terriers. Swift, simple, and uncomplicatedly brutal when the occasion demanded. The ground in which they played in those days looked very unusual. Bramall Lane was bounded by terracing on only three sides then, and just one stand was covered. Most people stood up to watch the game. Across the fourth side of the pitch you could see the Yorkshire County Cricket Ground sprawling away in a huge green oval. The cricket pitch began where the football pitch ended. This meant that shifting your allegiance from Sheffield United to the Yorkshire County Cricket Team during the summer months could not have been easier. So in June or thereabouts, Uncle Ken and I would enter through the turnstiles at the eastern end of Bramall Lane to watch fast bowler Freddie Truman roaring up to the crease. The men in red and white were replaced by the men in white.

Yes, much of Uncle Ken's life was given over to caring for me, to playing the part of a father. Then, as I grew, his influence upon me changed in character. I began to find myself increasingly preoccupied by the idea of him as a writer and what that might mean. From being a single, uncomplicated uncle, he gradually evolved into two persons in one.

And in time all that became immensely appealing to me, the idea of there being a separate person inside the person you were looking at, a partially mysterious someone who might be travelling in a slightly different direction from the man who had always walked away from you with such seemingly uncomplicated casualness.

A few weeks ago, I opened an old suitcase that my sister had discovered in my mother's attic in Totley some weeks after her death in 2009. Had this suitcase not been found, much of this memoir would have been unwritable. It would have been stuffed with undependable vagaries, subject to the whims of faulty memory. That small brown suitcase, a battered, pre-war model made from what looked like stiffened cardboard, had once belonged to my mother's second husband, Wilf Welsby. I remember him once having it in his hand. It seemed to partner well the trilby hat he was wearing on his head, cocked at a slighty jaunty angle. He was a relatively short man, Wilf Welsby, bowed of leg, and this small suitcase made him look business-like in a raffish, foot-in-the-door sort of way. At some point – perhaps after his death - my mother had filled that suitcase with my long abandoned belongings – goodness how I came to abandon or forget all these notebooks and drafts of bad poems from my teenage years.

When I opened the suitcase, there they all were, embarrassing witnesses to my struggle with the art of writing. One notebook, fuller, more coherent, and less tediously self-absorbed than much else, took me to the heart of my later relationship with Uncle Kenneth. I must have been about eighteen years old when I wrote about him, part way through my painful abandonment of the Christian faith. As usual, I was wrestling with the problems of becoming a writer. How do you do it? How do you get better at it? By this time my uncle had left home – he married my Aunt Ena, and said goodbye to his bachelor life at Coningsby Road, when I was sixteen years old – and was an increasingly rare visitor to the house. Here is the extract, written in fading pencil, rather awkwardly expressed, full of clumsy, anxious eagerness and slightly ridiculous self-importance – it is as if I am trying to talk myself up in my own eyes. I have not tried to tidy it up in any way. When I read it again, more than forty years after writing it, I was jolted into remembering that at some point I must have read at least a part of the novel that my uncle later destroyed in a fit of frustration and disappointment.

'I walked down from school at dinner time and made a resolve to increase my vocabulary. I came to this decision partly by reading my uncle's work and partly by my study of *Sons and Lovers* which has such a great diversity of vocabulary. On my way down the hill I set myself the task of giving their proper titles to trees, flowers and objects. I was informed by my mother at tea that Ken was paying a visit tonight which pleasantly surprised me. My having read his manuscript over the last few days has elevated him considerably in my sight, and I experienced a strange *élan* when he walked in the door. I suppose that I expected him to divulge the innermost secrets of his heart, and dazzle me with his limitless knowledge, but as always he was merely his pleasant rather conforming self. Later in the evening however I succeeded in steering the conversation round to writing and the novelist's art, introducing the theme by way of a comment upon D.H. Lawrence, whom my uncle idolizes. He came out with several rather profound statements upon art – the writer becomes the sensitivity of all those who cannot and do not write. He stated that he considered it sacrilege for a writer to crush the germ of creativity within him, and told me definitely that he was going to set to work writing again. This produced a strange effect upon me, bringing tears to my eyes. Again I feel that I need to cast off the superficial approach which I seem to be adopting towards life and study at the moment. It is only by dint of hard work and patient grind that I will achieve anything which is worthwhile, I am sure. I have not yet resolved the religious difficulties which continue to well up within me, though I am determined that even if I do find myself deciding to become an atheist, I should not become the frivolous, immature, unstudious youth I was before I ever became embroiled in the Christian faith. How difficult it is to know what it is right to do. I must be the personification of Indecision - no fixed ideas, no steady girl friend, no consistent opinion upon vital topics. I trust that I will be able to find a satisfactory balance, a mature balance, so that I may not be swayed by emotive language, but may be able to think out the different factors involved in a particular circumstance before resolving a definite plan of action.'

Life at Coningsby Road changed dramatically when I was sixteen years old. It was during this year that my uncle got married. By now my sister Pat was married too. Within the space of two years, we were down from six to four. The dynamics were changed. It was a less bustling, a less noisy place altogether. The possibility of sleeping in a small bedroom without the company of other people shuffling and coughing and fidgeting far into the night, offered itself to me like a very precious, hitherto undreamt of gift. New years of isolation in a room of one's own, the possibility of withdrawal to a quiet and sequestered spot, far enough away from the rest of the family, a place to think and dream and scheme – all this, of a sudden, became a reality to me. First of all, I stayed in the back bedroom, which I had shared with my uncle and a single chamber pot, which tended to live beneath his bed. I put my maps on the walls, one of which showed me the states of America and its national parks. I used to stare long and hard at Yellowstone National Park because that was where Yogi Bear lived. And then, to the wall directly above my head I attached an elegant map of New Zealand with its two islands, showing its physical contour lines, which meant that I could imagine its mountain ranges and its plunging valleys. I liked the shape of this map. It was almost like a strangely deformed human being of sorts. Being on my own during those years of evangelical commitment meant that I could fully indulge my desire to be alone with God. I would kneel and pray beside the bed, fervently, often out loud, but in a whisper. I didn't want to be thought of as someone who talked to himself, because that would have meant that I had a screw loose. There were a number of those types out in the street already.

I acquired spiral-bound notebooks of my own, and began to pour bad poems into them, partly written by myself and partly ghost-written by all the other poets that I was reading. Many of these bad poems were partially written by T.S. Eliot. I was beginning to believe that to be a writer was my destiny. I tried to cultivate my talents. The fact that Kenneth was now away from the house meant that his visits became all the more special to me. In his absence, the idea of him as a writer increased in importance.

A changing city in a changing world. The thought, expressed like that, sounds platitudinous. And yet the reality of change is troubling, profoundly so. And so it was for my mother, who left Fir Vale at the beginning of the 1980s, when her side of Coningsby Road was demolished to make way for a road-widening scheme which was subsequently abandoned. Oh, the frivolous decision-making processes of town planners! She left for Totley, worlds away socially from Fir Vale, and I would like to tell you that she found contentment there. But no, she did not. She made the irreversible mistake of taking herself with her, and that self, as ever, was full of suspicion, rancour and an unswerving belief that only family would sustain her. There was, as ever, unquantifiable menace just beyond the kitchen window. And Fir Vale itself changed beyond recognition. Other communities, from Asia and Africa, moved in, and reinvented this poor white quarter by turning it into a poor Asian and African quarter. My mother, who went back to Fir Vale occasionally in order to stoke her fury and her resentment, loathed what had happened. She could no longer recognise herself in that place. Everything that she once was had been erased. The process was inevitable, as inevitable as the fact that the past - any past - must make way for the present. The incomers were not to be blamed for being there. They were not illegal immigrants. They were from countries of the Commonwealth, citizens of our former colonial possessions. We had profited by what their country had to offer us. We had a duty to care for them. And so in they moved, and the houses and the shops, though still often physically present as before, changed utterly in character. New fruits, new vegetables appeared on the pavement fruit stands, strange, colourful stuffs that my mother would never have recognised as legitimate, let alone edible. Two years ago, as she lay dying in the Northern General Hospital - yes, fate and the NHS dictated that she was to die within a quarter of a mile of her old home in Coningsby Road - I walked those streets again, trying to re-find vestiges of what I too once had been. I walked through Fir Vale, down Owler Lane, past the spot where the redundant and derelict Methodist chapel used to be - there were so many defunct Methodist chapels within walking distance of Coningsby Road, almost as many chapels as there were dead or dying cinemas - past where Gregory's the baker used to stand sentinel on its corner site, with its odoriferous offerings of two ounces of potted meat in greaseproof paper and its tiny Hovis loaves that could be eaten in two or three bites.

I then walked on eastwards in the direction of where the steel works had once been until I eventually reached the road that led up to Wincobank Hill, that hillside which once overlooked the horrors and the splendours of the Don Valley, with its soot-blackened rolling mills and its intermittent spewings of flame from factory chimneys. I tried to find the track which would lead me directly uphill to the Second World War gun emplacement where I used to stand and survey all that once mighty industry, now, for the most part, long gone. This hill meant so much to me as a boy and a young man. At first it was the physical challenge of climbing it and of discovering what there was to be seen from its summit. Then, much later on, it began to take on a kind of symbolic force, and I planned a cycle of poems (all unwritten) about its past and its present.

By 2009, forty years on, this hill which I had known so well had changed almost beyond recognition. When I walked it as a boy, it was near-barren ground, tawny as a lion's pelt in colour. You could survey it in its entirety from close to the summit. There was a small estate of prefabs on the Western slope - it was from one of these prefabs that I once bought my first small, second-hand record player, the very Dansette on which I remember playing a prized copy of Bob Dylan's *Another Side* in 1964, purchased from an enterprising furniture shop in Rotherham. Otherwise, the only vegetation on those slopes were some hardy dwarf oaks. By 2009, on the afternoon that I absented myself from the Northern General Hospital in Fir Vale - there were several long hours to be killed between one set of visiting hours and the next - that hill side had changed utterly. From a distance - I had first seen it from Barnsley Road as, descending the hill, I surveyed the scene from the upper deck of the bus - I could see, to my astonishment, that Wincobank Hill, once so barren, was now as densely choked with trees as any small mountain in the Catskills. Could this really be true?

Yes, it was true all right. As soon as I reached the top of the hill, I saw, to my astonishment, that I could recognise almost nothing of what I could still remember of my 1960s' prospect of the Don Valley. Where had that terrible pall of smoke gone? Now that the industrial pollution caused by the steel industry was a thing of the distant past, nature had comprehensively re-claimed that hillside. The gun emplacement, with its tall brick staircase and circular brick top around which I had once run round and round and round like a mad eye, had disappeared too. I could not even find the site of my old vantage point. All this was both troubling and exhilarating. I was pleased that the soot which used to fall on my mother's washing from the skies was there no longer - I remember how she used to run out into the back yard, gather up the clean white sheets into her arms, and race back indoors - but I also felt a strong sense of personal loss when I realised that this was no longer the hill side of my boyhood. It was a different hill side now, a different place altogether. It now belonged to others.

The sight across the Don Valley had changed utterly too. The old, soot-blackened steelworks, the rolling mills, those hulking buildings of an extraordinarily monumental presence when you looked at them from the top deck of the bus as it chuntered along Attercliffe Common to Rotherham, had almost completely vanished, along with the generations of labouring men who had worked there.

I remember one of them so well. He lived next door but one to us in Coningsby Road, in a house which opened out into the next back yard to ours, just a few yards away. It would have been a matter of flinging a quick, short-trousered leg over a high wall, having first jumped up onto the neighbour's battered dustbin lid. I knew his daughter, Enid, she was one of my playmates. We spent hours together, playing hop skotch and such like in the street. But I never spoke to her father, and he never looked as if he was ever inclined to speak to a mere child like me. He wore a cap, a long, scruffy overcoat, and a dirty white muffler wound around his neck. His face looked set in stone. He was utterly unsmiling. He barely seemed to be aware of the world that surrounded him. I never saw him exchange a word with another human being. It was his task to travel down to the steelworks on the bus, do his shift, and then, utterly exhausted, return home and slump into a chair in front of the fire. That, it seemed to me, was his worldly lot. And I never heard anything said of him that would prove this to be untrue. He must have died when he reached his allotted span.

I, a mere self-preoccupied child, thought little about those men who were living such hard working lives in those days, in the steel works or down the coal mines. It was only later that they began to impinge upon me, when I understood what sacrifices these men had made to earn a modest living. Yes, it was because of the conditions in which they worked that the sign which read 'No Spitting' was displayed so prominently on the trams. If your lungs were not choked with the phlegm caused by industrial pollution, why would you have this constant urge to spit? The pavements of Fir Vale were covered in these tiny white flecks of dried spit. Spitting had nothing whatsoever to do with uncouthness. When the father of my friend Norman, a former coal miner, died of emphysema, smoking was not to blame. Blame years of hard work in a life-threatening environment.

Yes, the Don Valley of yesteryear, that terrible Blakean vision of industry run amock across this once green and pleasant land, had vanished utterly. And Wincobank Hill itself was now tree-filled, and even seemed to possess luscious meadows of grass. And yet, in spite of the fact that it now had more the look of a nature reserve than the barren tract of hillside I had remembered from my youth, it did not feel a happy place of general recreation. There was scarcely anyone about, no walkers, no families. Council estates now butted up to its edges, surrounded by harsh high fencing. At least one ferocious dog barked at me from behind a wall. There was such potential here, I felt, and such neglect too.

That feeling only intensified when I walked back through Fir Vale itself. Fir Vale now felt sadly unkempt and uncared for, neither fully alive nor fully dead. Houses were boarded up. Random demolitions had taken place in terraced streets that were once complete. It looked as if a mad dentist had had his way inside a helpless victim's mouth, wrenching out teeth here and there for no particular reason. I walked along Skinnerthorpe Road, an old haunt. There were once allotments behind this street where families could cultivate crops of potatoes, radishes and lettuces and, wherever it chose to take hold, vigorously colourful, tough-minded rhubarb plants grew with wild and ferocious abandon. Those allotments were long gone. Broken glass and rubble lay scattered about the streets at random. What could be done about any of this? I felt wholly at a loss to propose any solution. Meanwhile, my mother was dying in the Northern General Hospital. I felt as if I were grieving twice over, once for her, but also for myself too because I had lost a significant part of my own identity. My memories had been wholly set adrift from the sad realities of the present day. Fir Vale and I now seemed to be floating, hand in hand, on perilous seas.

Getting About

My great-grandmother, Mabel's mother, used to walk into town. That was the way you did it in those days, you used your legs. By the time I was born, it was trams you took up Barnsley Road towards the city centre. I loved trams, the way you could jump on after they'd started moving - they were never fast - clinging on to the pole at the back. Best of all was looking up at the rods that joined the tram to the electric cables, watching them spark, and listening to them fizzing and crackling - a bit like chips in a pan. They were funny, lurching beasts, trams, suddenly speeding up, then slowing down, or turning in elegant circles, like dancers twirling in a musical by Busby Berkeley, at the terminus. I liked the top deck best because you could see stuff from up there. I loved getting to Lady's Bridge in town, where the brewery hung over the weir, smelling the sweet stink of hops as you passed over the bridge, and looked down into the roaring river water. It was so fuggy with fag smoke on the top deck though, that was the only problem, that you could hardly see to see, and fag smoke choked up your throat. It got on your shoes as well, all those little heaps of grey ash. There wasn't any spitting on trams though. That's because you were told not to. NO SPITTING, it said. It was all over the pavement instead, gobby, little white patches. They were forever hawkin and spitting, blokes, when they came back from night shifts at Steel, Peach and Tozer down Attercliffe. They were dead rough down there, my mum always said. They didn't know any better, that sort.

Christmas Day

There was nothing quite like Christmas at Coningsby Road. Christmas Day was the most hallowed and special of days. It began well before dawn, in the middle of the night, when I would lie awake, practically breathless with excitement. I knew the rituals of Christmas. I knew that things would be going on in the front room on Christmas Eve, and that I would be forced to sit, marooned, kicking my legs, in the brightly lit kitchen as paper and string and tape were passed from hand to hand and mysteriously spirited elsewhere. Never you mind! Keep your nose out of other folks' business! That's what would be said whenever I asked, my enquiries abruptly cut off by nods and winks and smiles and mock- crossness and finger wagging. I liked it when people played at being cross. Then I'd be hurried upstairs to bed much too early because there were yet more things to be done downstairs, mysterious re-arrangings of this and that in preparation for the big day.

Best and worst of all were the early morning hours, before it got light, when I would stare at dawn nearly breaking until my eyes ached in their sockets, trying to control my overwhelming excitement as I lay there in bed. And then, at the appointed hour - it was probably as early as seven o'clock in the morning - Pat and I would be called down, and down we'd rush, falling over our own feet, shrieking and racing to overtake each other, always wanting to be first to see what there was to be seen. It was always the same, and though utterly ordinary in retrospect, it looked like the physical contours of a magical kingdom, the way our two white pillow cases, strangely bulging, were lying on the kitchen table, side by side. Then all the delving inside and the pulling out and the delicious tearing off of all that red and glittery Christmas paper would begin. We would finger the shapes, wondering aloud, and shouting out our guesses. The battery-driven Ack-Ack gun from Woolworth's, that would be one of the first to come out, and I would start on my gay killing spree almost immediately, swinging it wildly in the air, and watching how the yellow tube at the front would shuttle in and out as I listened to the wild noise of firing, and watched the sparks flying around the kitchen. Much more difficult to pull out because of its size would be the cardboard box of Bayko, which contained, I knew this already from what I had seen at other friend's houses, piles of tiny flat plastic bricks, red, blue or yellow, and short metal rods with which you would assemble the walls of houses and other kinds of buildings. The pillow case always seemed inexhaustible. It was as if the marvellous finding of new Christmas gifts might go on forever - and, similarly, you could not really believe that

79

the special day itself would not go on forever as well.

What was jarring, always, was going out of doors after it was all over indoors, gifts strewn about everywhere, unruly scraps of torn paper engulfing every surface. Yes, it was then, wrapped in a winter coat, that we would go out of doors for a walk in the chill of the alien air, and it was then that the strangeness and that slight, deflating sense of disappointment would start to seize hold. How could it be, I always asked myself as I sniffed the air of outdoors and took the hand of my mother in my own gloved hand, how could it be that this world beyond the door of the warming magic of our Christmas kitchen, was so like the out-of-doors world of yesterday, where all the normal things were happening? How was it that the outside did not seem to partake of the excitement of inside? How could the world have let us down so badly? Even the people out there, walking up and down Herries Road, attending to their own business, and especially the unsmiling adults wholly unknown to me – how could they not be smiling fit to crack their faces in half on this day of all days? - seemed not to be sharing the delirium I was experiencing inside myself. How could that be? Had they not too been given gifts? No, in order to re-discover the reassurance I craved that the world was wholly in tune with my own magical feelings, I had to run back indoors and turn on the radio or the television. The world of radio and television was celebrating my Christmas all right! All those dancing girls in their Christmas hats, laughing, hopping from side to side on one leg and kicking out like fury, knew about my gifts. They knew that my Christmas mood would never end until, all of a sudden, some time in the late evening, I was hit by such an overwhelming attack of happy tiredness that my mother had to scoop me up in her arms like an ungainly, strangely shaped Christmas parcel, and drop me into bed.

Religious Stirrings

I feel slightly queasy when I see this word at the head of a chapter. There was no religion to be had at 45 Coningsby Road during my childhood. No one prayed to God. No one offered him thanks for the trays of scones and the two apple pies - there were always just two baking trays - that my mother and my grandmother Mabel baked at the table in that hot kitchen, rain or shine, on Sunday afternoons. No small boy whispered thanks, eyes raised ceiling-ward, for the right to wipe clean the mixing bowl of that deliciously clarty yellow remnant of flour, eggs, butter and sugar that never failed to overload several smeary finger ends. Mild-mannered Jehovah's Witnesses may have come to the door from time to time, dressed in their dark hats and their over-heavy Sunday clothes on a week day, but no one gave them any time or credence. In fact, God only entered the house - and then only as an expletive - in the course of the regular Money Wars between my mother and my grandfather. Was there a Bible or two in the house? Yes, there was a New Testament, tucked away in a drawer somewhere as a faint memory of someone's past. But balancing that casual example of routine piety from yesteryear (it was my grandmother's, printed in the 1920s; I still have it) was another book which came to stir me mightily during my late-teenage years. I am referring to a battered paperback copy of Tom Paine's *The Age of Reason*, written at the dying end of the eighteenth century, which I happened upon one day in the tall boy of the front bedroom, keeping company with a much consulted copy of *Lady Chatterley's Lover* whose spine was broken at one of the smutty bits.

I still own Paine's ferocious and fearless denunciation of the Bible, its brilliant attacks upon its chronological absurdities. And it meant so much to me when I first came across it because at the time I was a fervent Christian, and Paine's book, so fearless, so unflinchingly courageous for then or any other time, terrified me to such an extent that I believed it to be the work of Satan himself.

Someone that I called God entered my life at the age of thirteen. I had joined the Scripture Union at Firth Park Grammar School. It was run by a swarthy, thick-set man called David Smith, who was head of the French Department, and had an intimidating habit of running full pelt beside the boys down the soccer pitch, slowly edging them off the ball by the sheer force of his speed and his weight. Daz Smith, in collusion with the headmaster, would invite his friend Gordon Sergeant to preach to us at school. This happened during school hours. Yes, an evangelical was allowed to run amock amongst vulnerable children with the blessing of the headmaster! Sergeant was an itinerant evangelist who wore, I was quick to notice, a different suit every day, and very good, highly polished brown shoes. How had he come by such wealth? This intrigued me. I was told that God alone provided for him. He would pray, and God would slip coins sufficient unto the day into his well tailored pockets. He had no other source of regular income. Sergeant was an impressive man, with a winning smile and a set of extraordinarily regular teeth - unlike almost everyone else in Sheffield. We were seduced and utterly won over by him. Though strikingly sharp-suited, he seemed so at one with us. He flashed us boyish, companionable smiles as he swung his Bible through the air to illustrate a point. It strikes me now that he was a forerunner of the televangelist phenomenon, but I knew of no such men in those days.

But that was not all. In those days Firth Park Grammar School was alive with Christian conviction on the rampage. Each summer David Smith would take a party of boys to Pioneer Camp at Benllech Bay on squally Anglesey, just off the north coast of Wales. There, in bell tents pitched a couple of fields back from the sea, hundreds of boy of a similar age - between about thirteen and seventeen - would be preached at night after night by another evangelical Christian called David Tryon. Tryon, a man from Lincolnshire in his early sixties, who wore knee-length khaki shorts and a brown Harris Tweed jacket with leather elbow patches, was a commanding presence amongst us, stern, firm, yet kind. One evening, I heard the call - and I responded. He had been preaching about Jesus as the Light of the World, of a Saviour who would willingly come and knock on the door of your heart, as the rain drove unremittingly against the walls of the marquee. I was invited to accept Jesus into my life as my personal saviour. I was promised an intimate, one-to-one relationship with the creator of the universe. The prospect struck me as quite extraordinary, unlike anything else that had happened to me in my life. I bowed my head and whispered Yes, Lord, come into my life.

At a stroke, everything had changed. My utterly ordinary existence as a child brought up in a terraced house in north-east Sheffield had been transformed. The story of my insignificant life had been re-written. Having been born a fatherless almost-nothing, a creature of importance only to my small and immediate family, I suddenly found myself, as if by chance (but, in fact, I was reassured in no uncertain terms, by the will of Providence), caught up in a universal drama that had extended through two millennia, and would continue to reverberate until Christ himself put a stop to it all at the Last Judgement, which may or may not take place any time soon. I suddenly found myself embroiled in something which touched every man, woman and child equally. The message of the gospel was of the utmost urgency, I quickly learnt, and I soon came to be regarded - and to regard myself - as one of the trusted custodians of that message. Jesus had died for us all, and unless we acknowledged that fact and acted upon it with the utmost speed, the consequences would be dire indeed. We would be lost forever. Nothing could be of greater importance.

I returned to that Christian camp on Anglesey during the summer of the following year to top up my dose of religious mania. Aside from Jesus with his lamp at the door of the heart and his ever beckoning finger, there were other forms of recreation on offer that I remember with some fondness. Open-air spud-bashing in a rain-lashed field, for example – the spuds would have to be chased around, and then scooped with freezing fingers, out of vats of cold water, lively and pocky with rain drops, before peeling. I had never known such fierce lashings of rain as I experienced at Benllech Bay. It was as if God knew in his heart of hearts that to broadcast his words most successfully, you needed the persuasive accompaniment of apocalyptic weather conditions. Or, at breakfast time, spooning up huge portions of gluey porridge from an aluminium vat, and then almost drowning them in milk and white sugar. Or, in a nearby field sucky with mud, wildly flinging a thick, green rubber ring over a badminton net, and hoping and praying as you did so that, if you had spun it backwards wildly enough, you would see it bounce out of your opponent's fumbling fingers, and then fall to the ground. Or going alone to the always-near-empty, small-shed-like cinema to watch Tony Hancock in *The Punch and Judy Man*, the sad tale of a man on the margins in a miserable seaside town not wholly unlike the one in which the cinema was situated. And then, most exquisitely punishing of all, doing the annual climb up Snowdon, Wales' highest mountain, for the sheer hell of testing young bodies to the utmost. Doing that climb was like climbing the slopes of hell itself. No matter where you put your uncertain feet, they would always seem to slip back half a step down muddy slurry half submerged by tiny, onrushing streams. For most of the climb you would be in the clouds, swathed in miserable swirls of mist and rain. You could see no more than a few yards ahead of you at any one time. And then, after hours of toil up the wildest and most unreliable of tracks, there would loom, wreathed in a semi-spectral mist, in all its ugly ingloriousness, the gloomy hotel on the mountain's summit. There can be fewer sights more bizarre than this one - to see a dreary looking hotel waiting for you after all that wildness. Yes, it seemed a terrible effrontery of sorts to be confronted all of a sudden by evidence of the human, but also a warm and welcome haven after so much leg-punishing, leg-numbing physical labour.

After gulping down hot tea, the descent would begin, down a track fit only for beasts aptly named the Pig Track, past marvellous, glittering inland lakes – the sun would peek out, tantalisingly, from time to time - so much water held suspended, as if by some miracle, so high in the hills. Like water held in a bowl, above head height, by the tallest of tall men.

   In August of 1962, I bought a postcard in that hotel – it is stamped 'Summit of Snowdon' in blue – and posted it back to my sister in Coningsby Road, having carried it all the way down the mountain in the pocket of my anorak. Here is what that thirteen-year-old boy in the Lord wrote to her, years before Gore-Tex changed the lives of those who are obliged to toil up mountains in the mist and the driving rain.

'Dear Pat,
Sorry for the soggy postcard. Arrived at the bottom of Snowdon about 1 o'clock. All the way up it was a very hard, sheer climb, and all the time it was thundering, absolutely pouring with rain, and blowing a gale. I had on my anorak and 2 pullovers a shirt and a vest. When I got to the top I took of [sic] my vest and rung [sic] it out. All the way down you had to walk through rivers and by the time I got to the bottom I was absolutely drowned and had to change everything. Love Mick xxxx '

   What else did we do when we were not either protecting ourselves from the rain, flinging rubber hoops over a net in a soggy field, or fervently praying to the Saviour in tiny, intense huddles? We would take the coach to a railway station elsewhere on Anglesey in order to do nothing but buy the platform tickets which were proudly on sale there. In those days, you had to buy a platform ticket - they usually cost a few old pennies – to gain access to the platform of a railway station if you wished to do a bit of train-spotting. Train- spotting was an awe-inspiring pursuit in the era of steam. It was the equivalent of a day out, to be taken to a mainline station. As a child, I would regularly be taken, accompanied by my Uncle Kenneth, to one of the two stations in Sheffield – the Midland (which served trains coming up from the South) or the Victoria, just beside the Wicker Arches (whose trains carried lucky travellers, never me, across the wildness of the Pennines to Manchester) - merely in order to see the drama of huge steam trains clanking and hissing and roaring through the station, all pistons churning, as they belched out steam and great potherings of black smoke. They were always so enormous and so black, these trains, quite terrifying in their power to deafen and to crush us. Except that they never could quite crush us because they were always safely confined to the tracks along which they moved, so surprisingly smoothly, thank goodness. So we would pay one or two pennies for a platform ticket, dropping our money into the machine and then, ticket tight clenched in hand, just go and look at them, standing there snorting like some great beast or passing deafeningly through, and let ourselves feel terrified by their mighty, daunting presences.

It was a little different at that station on Anglesey. I do not remember ever having seen a single train there. It always felt too quiet for trains. More suited to bird song perhaps. Why be taken there then, by coach, part way across the island from our camp near the beach? We went there in order to buy precious samples of the platform tickets on sale at that place alone. I remembered this all of a sudden when I rooted through the old brown suitcase that my mother had kept in her loft. I discovered four – yes, four! - of these tickets, all identical to each other. And we had gone there expressly to buy them because they were the longest platform tickets in the world – just as this tiny railway station had the distinction of being the one with the longest name, we were always assured, in the world: LLANFAIRPWLLGWYNGLLGOGERYCHWYRNDROBWLLLLAN-TYSILIOGOGOGOCH. I can recite it as a party piece to this day.

Yes, I returned home from that first camp with a kind of fire burning inside of me. I had known nothing like it before. I felt full to brimming over with something wonderful and strange. It was an experience, I quickly came to recognise, wholly alien to everyone that I had ever known. And yet I knew it to be true for myself and others too. I had no doubts about that whatsoever. How could I enlighten the lost, educate the sinners? The single most extraordinary aspect of this relatively short-lived evangelical phase of my life was that sense of inner security I had suddenly been granted. It had come winging its way down through the air as if from nowhere. I no longer felt myself to be a thing tossed about by the whim of a breeze. I was deep-rooted at last, like that major oak in Sherwood Forest I saw for the first time as a teenager. And yet, unlike that great tree, I did not depend for my survival, here and hereafter, upon supports fashioned by mere men. God alone sustained me, and he was more than sufficient.

Nothing had changed back at Coningsby Road. The old rancours still persisted. Rain still streamed down the window panes. Soot still sullied my mother's sheets out in the back yard. My sister Pat was still working as a shorthand typist in the offices of Firth Vickers steelworks on Savile Street. There were still dripping sandwiches for tea at 5 o'clock in the afternoon. That was an awkward period for me. I belonged in that house, it was my home, and yet the spiritual part of me no longer belonged there. I felt myself to be a kind of stranger in that oh-so-familiar place.

God had called me to higher things, and I could not have been more convinced of that fact. But it also became apparent to me, quite quickly, that if I were to continue to thrive as a Christian, I would need the companionship of fellow believers. I had a great fear of losing what I had already won, that precious relationship with the Saviour himself. Did I not owe it to the Man who had died for me on Calvary's tree to do my best for him? I needed to concentrate on spiritual things in order not to be distracted by the everyday. I fervently wished to convert my own family, to share with them my enthusiasm for what I knew, to acquaint them with the gravity of their situation as lost sinners. But when I looked at them, they seemed to be both completely unknowing and wholly indifferent. They had no inkling of what they were missing. They didn't disapprove of my new found religious beliefs, not at all. I felt that they tiptoed around me, acquiescing in my new self without at all wishing to enter into it or even to understand it. It was an embarrassment to me, this impasse. These people were my relatives, my elders. Should I presume to tell them that they were wrong about their lives? I could not find the words to do it, so I hit on what I regarded as more subtle tactics. At meetings I attended I was often given tracts, small booklets which described the fundamentals of the Christian faith for the non-believer. One of these small booklets, a blue one, was called, quite simply, *How to Become a Christian*. One day I left a copy of it on the kitchen table. It remained there throughout the day. When, at some point in the late afternoon, my mother was dusting the crumbs from the table in preparation for tea, I nudged it gently in her direction and smiled at her rather weakly. She told me that she thought it looked quite interesting, love. That was as close as I ever came to acquainting my mother with the fact that she was running, hell for leather, down the road to perdition.

I sought out other true believers, all over the city. By then, I had become aware of another startling fact. Though painfully shy, I became less so when I was sharing this knowledge of my new- found faith with others. It was as if a different person was speaking in my place, more confident, more socially assured. Surely it was Jesus who was speaking through me. It would simply not have happened without the aid of the Saviour of the World. My messianic zeal increased by leaps and bounds. I joined the local Trinity Fir Vale Methodist Church, although I sensed in my teenage all-knowingness that there were few true believers amongst its congregation. Perhaps it was part of my task to enlighten the churchgoer. I spent Saturday evenings at Assembly of God revival meetings in the auditorium at the rear of the City Hall, listening to the stirring voices of the young gospel choir and to the short, fiery, bespectacled preacher. I read more than I had ever read in my life: the Bible, biblical commentaries, Dietrich Bonhoeffer's *Letters and Papers from Prison*, Thomas a Kempis' *Imitations of Christ*... I became, in time, head of the local Sunday School at Trinity Fir Vale Methodist Church. I sang simple-minded choruses to the accompaniment of my twelve-string guitar at Sunday afternoon Pathfinder groups in the local church, and in front of Sheffield Cathedral during Christian Aid Week. I spent weekday evenings at Bible study groups. I became head of the Scripture Union. I prayed in school, before lessons began, huddled with other true believers on the back stairs behind the classroom where, later in the day, I would listen to the blasphemous poems of the syphilitic Charles Baudelaire being read out loud by a histrionic poet *manqué* who was wasting his life as a teacher in the French department of a grammar school. Had I known then what I later came to discover about Charles Baudelaire, I would have squirmed with guilt as I listened to his words. Something else of great future significance to me was beginning to happen. I was falling in love with the art and the craft of poetry.

Christianity disappeared from my life almost as suddenly as it had appeared. For about three or four years, I was passionately committed to it. I kneeled beside my bed every night. I read the Bible assiduously and such sustaining books as *The Christian's Secret of a Happy Life*. I felt firm in the conviction that I was on the true path. Then, relatively suddenly, and as I aged and matured, that superstructure began to fall away. Reading played its part. For a long time I had tried to shield myself from the influence of writers who were sworn enemies of the Christian religion. Whenever I picked up a book which seemed to challenge the veracity of Christian dogma by the likes of Jean-Paul Sartre or Albert Camus, I felt stung to the quick, angered, frightened. I fought back by reading rebuttals of such books by equally fervent apologists for the Christian faith, but, little by little, the opponents began to get the better of the argument. One day, I asked myself a question which I knew was fundamental to everything that I believed. Here is how I put that question to myself. How do you know that the dogmas of Christianity are true? And if you do not know for certain that they are true, why are you living as though they were? You are basing your life on a lie. I could not fight back against that diabolical interrogator. I began to back-slide - which is how the evangelical Christian describes a former believer who is beginning to lose touch with his faith.

The experience of falling away from this all-embracing faith troubled me deeply. It had been my life, my reason for being. Most of my closest friends were of the same persuasion. I remember one particular afternoon as I stood on the landing of the old turret building at the heart of Firth Park

Grammar School, being jostled by boys. I experienced a terrible sense of vertigo as I waited on the turn of the stairs just outside the headmaster's office. I felt as if I was falling, falling unstoppably, into a bottomless abyss. No one would be there at the bottom to catch me. There would never be anyone there. I later wrote a rather bad poem about this experience which was published in the school magazine. That poem - the best of it is in its title - was called 'Interior Subsidence'. Worse was to yet to come.

Most of my friends were Christians. I talked to them, I ate with them, I socialised with them, I worshipped with them. But after I came to recognise that Christianity was beginning to mean less and less to me, my relationship with these people became uncomfortable. I remember one particular afternoon in the summer of 1968. I was soon to leave Sheffield for a new life at university. I was spending some time with old friends, fervent Christians who owned a shop selling wallpaper at Burngreave. I was sitting in the kitchen with the mother of the family. I explained my predicament to her. I told her that I was finding it increasingly difficult to believe in Christian doctrine, and that my old friends were being unsympathetic. I expected her to be kind to me, to offer me words of consolation. She looked at me with the utmost coldness and said: 'Well, Michael, if you come where the fire's burning, you must expect to get burnt.' I was so taken aback by the harshness of her words that I couldn't reply. I left the house on Osgathorpe Close soon after that. It was as if this woman had hit me in the face. I felt bruised. I told no one at home. What would have been the point? At best they had tolerated my weird spiritual adventures.

Later, I had a dream that I was sitting in her kitchen, and that she was saying those very words to me all over again. Once again I was saying nothing in response. I woke up feeling miserable, frightened. Then I remembered that the dream had been true after all. That response to my 'falling away' was not unusual. I discovered that a believer and an unbeliever are separated by a mighty, unbridgeable gulf. Far better, I felt, if I had never believed at all. Then, at least, there might have been hope for me.

Stanley

Abstractions do not count. We are in the grip of particular human beings. They shape our lives. They make us what we are. Social forces are as nothing by comparison with the chance encounter. I drifted through most of my six or seven years as a boy at Firth Park Grammar School. I always did well enough. To do well was quite sufficient. Then, quite late on in my school career, much to my surprise, I began to do much better than well.

A chance encounter with a remarkable teacher caused me not only to change direction, but to discover something about myself which I did not know existed. I met Stanley Cook when I studied English Literature in the last two years of my school life. I had always taken him to be a fairly unremarkable man, someone easily overlooked, who cared nothing about making an impression upon the world. I knew that he lived in a house with a steep front garden on Barnsley Road, which was on my punishing, daily cycle route up hill to school. I would see him as I cycled by, a balding, slightly glum looking man with a comb-over, in a long and rather shapeless black overcoat, carrying a saggy leather bag full, I didn't doubt, of school exercise books. His face always looked strangely expressionless, as if he lived deep inside himself. He didn't look at me. We never exchanged a word. I was one more local boy amongst more than seven hundred others. And he was yet another teacher, appointed to do what teachers are paid to do.

I first came across him face to face, day after day, when I opted to do English at 'A' level. He taught me literature. He introduced me to Milton, Arnold, Shakespeare, Swift, that pantheon of literary heroes. His manner of speaking was enthralling. I had never heard anyone talk like this man. His delivery was bland, slightly hesitant, and discouragingly unemphatic. He would express an opinion in an utterly matter-of-fact way, as if what he was saying was relatively inconsequential. His face would be dead pan, humourless, almost without expression. As he spoke, relatively slowly - he never seemed to be in a hurry to speak - he would gently chop at the top of the desk in front of which he was sitting with the side of his right hand, following that hand with his eye as if it possessed the key to our future comprehension. Directly in front of him there would probably be a green school exercise book identical to the ones which in due course we would be filling with our dictation and our homework. In it there would be very brief and well organised notes, often numbered, about the book we were discussing, written by himself.

What took me by surprise, always, was that the meaning of what he was saying seemed to be at odds not only with the words that he was using, but with his manner of delivery too. He was gently exercising the art of irony. I had never heard language used in this way, so calculatedly, with such restrained, humorous precision. He would go through poems and gobbets of prose with us, word by word, prising them apart, raising up words, syllables, entire sentences for our particular delectation, demonstrating to us how language could be used as a weapon of argument, persuasion, seduction. Poetry came alive for me as it never had before. Stanley himself, I soon discovered, was a remarkable poet in his own right - his first full-length book was just about to be published. That book, *Signs of Life*, contains many of his best poems. Little by little, we became friends. We exchanged poems as we wrote them, inviting comments. I visited his house on Barnsley Road. We discussed each other's poetry. He was the first living, practising poet I had ever met, the first poet who showed me by his example how words could define a place, a group of people, a very particular atmosphere. Stanley, for his time, defined the contours of Sheffield, that elusive city of my birth. He helped to bring the city alive for me, imaginatively. This book that I am writing is one of the late fruits of those conversations in his front room on Barnsley Road in front of a roaring gas fire, decades ago. I still hear that slightly sceptical voice of his inside my head, picking words apart as if with a fine, well honed blade.

After Stanley's death in 1991, I was invited back to that house by his widow, Kathleen, to choose from amongst his books. It was one of the most painful afternoons of my life, seeing this interior that I had known so well, and that I had visited so often, being dismantled before my very eyes, as if it were a stage set or some other temporary human contrivance. The book shelves, once full to bursting, were now half empty. The chairs were no longer in their customary places. I could now see very clearly that the walls and the ceiling were stained yellow from years of smoking short cigars. Most of all, Stanley himself was no longer there, clever, hesitant, awkward, slightly shabbily dressed, to discuss the art of poetry with me. Stanley was generally in the habit of claiming ownership of his books by inscribing them with his name. Kathleen told me that she had carefully gone through all of those books, one by one, cutting out Stanley's signature with a pair of scissors. Yes, she had mutilated all Stanley's books, and with the very best of intentions. Perhaps it had upset her to think that something so personal as a signature might travel elsewhere, far beyond the reach of their long married life.

Stanley

So much of life is pure serendipity. There were other English teachers at that school, senior to Stanley. Dr F.T. Wood, a thin, tall man who was never to be seen without his black cloak thrown across his shoulders as a not-so-subtle way of emphasising his eminence and his seniority amongst the teaching staff, was the first of these, and the only one who has stuck in my memory. Though a well published author of books about English grammatical idioms - Macmillan published those books, which is an indication of his relative importance within that bleak field - he was an object of relentless mockery. The sign board above his classroom door had been deftly amended to read DRIFTWOOD, and that is exactly what he seemed to us, a lank and bony agglomeration of ridiculous affectations, which was most in evidence in his voice, which had a sing-song, horribly repetitive reediness about it. It was as if every word that he uttered somehow had got stuck half way up his nose. We mocked and ragged him mercilessly, banging all our wooden desk lids simultaneously when his back was turned for the sheer pleasure of seeing him jump and wince with near impotent fury. Then out would come his thin, flexible cane. I can hear now how it whistled down through the air before it connected with my finger ends. I remember walking back to my desk at the back of the room - I always preferred to sit at the back for the possibilities of unremarked distraction that it always offered me - squeezing my hands together to relieve the stinging pain.

For all his knowledge of grammatical niceties, Driftwood was a terrible teacher precisely because he was who he was. He knew his course, and he adhered to it, unflinchingly. He had no way of controlling a class of ragged boys with an insatiable appetite for unruliness. He had no ability to bend to the needs of the individual. We were who we were, and what we had always been, cussed boys who were there to be corralled and, if possible, trained a little. The goal was unattainable, he knew that. We were too savage by half. He taught us *The Merchant of Venice* by obliging us to take it in turns to read, speech after speech, out loud, to him, stumbling as we went. I remember him reading parts of it to us in order to show us the way, and of the jeering that greeted him when he opened his mouth with its delicately spittle-flecked edges. Shakespeare, it became immediately apparent to all of us, was boring, irrelevant and dull. He had nothing to do with our present. And it was as if Driftwood, rocking there on his heels, in his mighty billowing black cloak, intoning speech after incomprehensible speech from on high in that ridiculously anachronistic voice of his, was knowingly taunting us for our lamentable ignorance of the higher things of life by introducing us to him. *The Merchant of Venice* is still my least favourite play by Shakespeare.

How is it that the greatest of English poets could be transformed,

91

within the space of a couple of years, from being a subject of complete indifference to me to one of intense fascination? What alchemy could do such a thing?

Reading and Writing

Writing is a form of addiction. Once you are addicted, it is extremely difficult to rid yourself of the writing habit. You write yourself into existence. Your thoughts are not fully or adequately articulated unless and until you have written them down. Quite often I do not know what I think about something - a painting, for example - until I have written about it. Writing is a voyage of self-discovery.

I discovered this for the first time, quite by chance one day, at Firth Park Grammar School, when we were all asked to write a story. I had no subject. I was staring helplessly out of the window, seeking inspiration in the bicycle racks. I did not know what that story would consist of nor where it would go, but as I began to write, I recognised, to my amazement, that the story, little by little, was writing itself. Perhaps another way to begin is by trying to express your raw feelings in words. This is how I came to the writing of poetry when I was about fifteen years old.

That early writing, crude marshallings of ringingly poetic words and phrases from here and there, was an attempt to situate myself in the world, to question why I was the person I believed myself to be, and what this unfolding idea of myself represented. If those early poems were often confusing and confused, that was because I myself was living in a state of the utmost confusion. For many people this is the meaning of poetry and its final end. Poetry is a kind of bursting forth. It is the raw outpouring of immediate emotion, which may have been provoked by something terrible or something wonderful. Death. First Love. This kind of writing seems to come from a place we might vaguely describe as the human heart. Sadly, that, at best, is the merest beginnings of poetry and not its end.

I was not a voracious reader of highly literary books when I was a child. I did not learn the name Arthur Ransome, that author so beloved of the middle classes, until I became an editor of children's books in the 1970s. The story I remember being read to me in my cot in the front bedroom was called 'Browny Biddles Boots' and it was written by Enid Blyton, a writer despised by parents with literary tastes. I adored her books. This story was about a pair of boots which decided to walk away from their owner, down a twisty lane, in the direction of magical lands. I listened to it over and over again, wondering about the fact that a mere pair of boots could have such an independent spirit. I read much else as a child, but my reading did not become a serious pursuit, something more than merely recreational, until religion took hold of me. I borrowed books voraciously from Page Hall Library, *Jennings, Just William, the Famous Five, the Secret Seven*. But the kind of reading I did later, under the influence of religion, was something wholly different. At this pivotal moment in my life, reading seemed to provide me with the key to a knowledge of the things for which I was thirsting: the nature of creation; the mystery of the redemption. Reading allowed me access to inner worlds. There, untrammelled by any physical location, I could roam freely, breathe the heady air of intellectual and emotional enquiry. Even though religion betrayed me in the end, it also opened a door to some of the profounder mysteries of life. It linked hands with later pursuits. It existed in the same inner space as poetry and Bob Dylan.

Motorbikes and Sideshows

Motorbikes played a large part in my young life at Coningsby Road. My grandfather owned several, though not simultaneously. When I was very young, his motorbike was very large - a 500cc BSA, with the hottest petrol tank I had ever accidentally touched. It often used to sit there out in the back yard, reared back on its stand, just outside the kitchen window, red petrol tank gleaming, like a tethered beast. By the time I had grown older and bigger, Harold's motor bike had shrunk to a green, 150cc Triumph.

I would watch my grandfather tinkering with his bikes out there in the backyard, half-smiling, half-scowling grimly, with his gleaming tools, unfurled from greasy rags, scattered at his feet, fingers all a squirmy black and sticky sheen. On good days, I would be allowed to ride pillion, helmetless, clinging to the leather belt of his huge brown coat, which always smelled of engine oil. No one saw anything wrong in that. Very early on, there had been a sidecar, a tiny, rickety, box-like thing into which my grandmother would squeeze herself like a large and swollen cake into a small cake box.

By the 1960s, my grandfather had shifted gear. He had bought a car, a gleaming maroon MG Magnette Saloon, with leather upholstery, tired and wrinkly to the touch, but still splendid in its way. Our half-used tin of Duraglit had never lovingly massaged such acres of chrome. This car was a sleek and purring thing over which I never ceased to marvel. When I sat in it, I turned into someone else, someone slightly more important than I had ever been before. We used to go for aimless drives, my grandfather, grandmother, Dorothy and I, on Sunday afternoons. We went nowhere in particular. We were driving just for the sake of it. We were motioing aimlessly along to show off our peacock of a second-hand car. I remember that we often used to make for the flatlands of north Lincolnshire, and to a particularly dreary little shop that sold ice cream of an indifferent quality. Was it on one of those trips that I drove a fully loaded ice cream cone into the back of my mother's neck? Perhaps. Boredom might have driven me to it. There we would sit, in a car park, quietly and malcontentedly slurping. I would be parked in the back, reading articles by the *Sunday Times* Insight team or editorials from the *Observer*, furiously half-alive elsewhere.

What I have failed to mention so far is that my family did not breed car drivers of any great distinction. My Uncle Kenneth drove well enough, but I could tell that he was not really engaged with the job in hand. After all, driving lacks imaginative potential. The road is usually a dreary, fixed place. You cannot suddenly take off into hinterlands of your own devising without courting the risk of a prison sentence. Consequently, he often seemed distracted when he drove, as if he was afloat on a cloud. Nothing calamitous ever happened, but I never felt entirely safe in his company either when he was driving a car. My grandfather was a breed of driver quite set apart from all the rest. Could this have been something to do with the fact that he had succeeded in surviving the worst that any war could have thrown at a man? Whatever the reason, my grandfather was the worst, most headstrong and most arrogant driver I have ever experienced in my life. It is his shining example, I fear, that has helped to turn me into a craven and spasmodic driver of indifferent quality. He would have no concern whatsoever for the rights of other users of the public highways. He barely recognised their presence. The road was his alone. Every other consideration was secondary. I remember driving into the centre of Sheffield one day. As we cruised downhill towards the Wicker Arches, I noticed that he seemed to be occupying an unusually challenging position in the road, mid way between the right-hand and the left-hand lanes. It would have been futile for me to raise an objection. I would have been slapped down for being inconsequentially young. Fortunately, my mother had noticed it too. When she pointed this fact out to him, all he said was: I'm straddlin' 'em both, Dorothy. That was by no means the worst of his misdemeanours. On that particular day other road sharers, in their wisdom, kept a wary distance.

Others were not so fortunate. Harold drove with a contemptuously breezy recklessness. One day we were in a car park in Blackpool. We were parked in one of two parallel lanes of cars, quite tightly packed together. As my grandfather reversed to leave, he yanked violently down on the right-hand side of the steering wheel for reasons known only to himself. The car just to the right of me - I was seated in the back - took a nasty scrape. Irritated that another car should have hindered his rapid backwards progress, my grandfather, swiftly and decisively correcting his desired angle of propulsion, shot forward, mauling the driver's door of the car to his left. Now in a state of advanced exasperation, he again adjusted the wheel until it was just so, and then rocketed backwards fifteen yards, squarely and forcefully hitting the bumper of the car that was parked directly behind us in an entirely different row of cars. One solution alone remained to us: to leave as rapidly as possible before the past caught up with the present. The best that can be said is that no human pain was caused as a result of these incidents.

A few days later, as we were silently cruising down Barnsley Road towards Fir Vale - my grandfather disengaged the gears from time to time when moving downhill in order to save on petrol consumption - he failed to notice the man who was walking confidently across a pesky pedestrian crossing. I heard the gentlest of jolts as a foot was run over. Had we not been accelerating away from the incident at such speed, I am sure that our ears would also have registered the squeals of pain, and we may even have witnessed an impotently raised fist.

School Life

School, for any child, is a terrible interruption in an otherwise perfect succession of days. My school life began well before the age of five, at Firs Hill Primary School, just a hundred yards from where a fellow Sheffielder called Peter Stringfellow founded his Mojo Club. I went up the hill to school on that first day in a judderingly slow tram with my mother, gripping her hand ferociously. What child ever wants a mother to leave on the first day of the rest of one's young life? Weeks later, I would be coming back on my own, sometimes running downhill all the way. The school itself was a rough and tumble sort of a place which stood half way up a small hill, side on to the beginnings of Roe Woods, where I would wander through carpets of bluebells in the springtime, and catch minnows in one of its seven small ponds. On one of my first days at school, I found myself penned inside what we would now call a makeshift attempt at a Wendy House by several tough and officious looking girls who were briskly setting up a functioning household of sorts with small, timorousness, confused males as slaves. They were expecting me to do menial jobs for them as they loud-mouthed it all over the place. A kindly girl with a wincingly ugly face who was busying herself nearby, making sweeping motions with a broom - perhaps she was destined to be a cleaner - protested at my incarceration, and I was quickly released. The best part of that new-built classroom were its huge picture windows. When inside, we could always keep a welcome eye on the world of the coming playtime outside. Generally speaking, I kept my head down. I observed fights from a safe distance. When I came a cropper on the steep street just outside the school gate, Miss Brown, newly qualified to console the bruised young, took me on her knee and let me sob away the pain. When seated at my old wooden school desk, feet thudding against its mighty, cast-iron frame, I remember spending a long time admiring the white, chipped ceramic ink well that fitted so perfectly into the hole at the top left-hand corner of my desk, and carefully dipping my glinting chrome pen nib into its murky blue waters, stirring just a little. I did my spelling and number exercises well enough. I listened, enthralled, as a teacher, fresh back from the war, without teaching qualifications of any kind, read *Treasure Island* by Robert Louis Stevenson out loud to us on Friday afternoons. I slurped at my sturdy, half pint glass bottle of milk at the beginning of playtime, leaving the usual rim of cream on upper and lower lip.

Harvest times came and went with vegetables and fruit, nestled in crepe paper, towering in mighty heaps on trestle tables in the school hall. Maps of the world on the classroom wall were slathered red wherever it seemed to matter, with England, small but forever mighty, pivoting about its centre. I also remember the text book which was used to teach us our history, ancient and modern all happily muddled altogether, of how ancient and battered it looked, and how curious its illustrations seemed to be. Straight out of the late nineteenth century, I would guess. The primitive peoples of the world had never looked more in need of our robust compassion. This book was an object of historical interest in its own right. Best of all was football out in the school yard, at break time, though I never excelled at it or any other game. Instead, I would secretly envy the dribbling skills of a small powerhouse of a boy called Michael Parkin, who would roll his black shorts up high and his socks down low, and then dribble past us all like a swivelling, swerving meteorite. What has stayed with me longest (I still find myself humming it from time to time) is a snatch of an aria from Handel that we sang en masse in the school hall, conducted by Mr Cox, the ancient head master: Where e'r you walk, cool glades shall fan the glades, trees where you sit shall crowd into a shade...' A minor poem, benignly set to music, had tiptoed into the frame of my young life.

The worst nightmares of my early school days were off-site trips to the school dentist for fillings. You could say that I had brought it upon myself by chewing too much Beach Nut chewing gum, sucking at too many gob stoppers, blissfully chomping down on too many chocolate-coated toffees, tearing apart one too many multi-coloured liquorice all-sorts of all shapes and sizes. The treatment was sadistic - there is no other word for it. According to this dentist from that bygone era, the greatest challenge when filling the tooth of a small child is to ensure that the mouth is kept fully opened at all times. In order to be sure that this happened, he would insert a hinged metal device which opened a child's mouth wider and wider, and then kept it open at that extremely painful angle until he had done all his endless fiddling and poking and drilling. And then there was the unforgettable day of the extraction of a decayed tooth, when a brown rubber mask was clamped over my mouth, and, rendered dreamily confused by ether, I found myself drifting away from myself down a long and echoing tunnel. Did I ever complain about any of this? No. My mother was seated outside in the corridor, patiently waiting, ever deferential towards authority.

When I look again at photographs of myself as a small boy at my first school, I feel deeply embarrassed to see quite how hen-pecked and mother-coddled I look, with my neat, v-neck sweater and my tiny, well-centred tie. I see the imprint of the clip in my hair to keep it from falling into my eyes, and I want to reach out and snatch it away. Why did I not become an object of mockery? What other child was forced to suffer the indignities of a grip in his hair! It is a wonder I ever grew up at all with a mother quite so suffocatingly overbearing as Dorothy. O that she had had other sources of distraction!

And then came Firth Park Grammar School, which existed for the education of boys alone, with its pompous, pollution-blackened turret, at the very top of which HJS Wilson the headmaster, ever imperious and mindful of his status (his full name, with its flourish of interlacing initials, is on every school report), and Mr Wetherill, his balding, stoop-shouldered and forever worried-looking deputy head, would emerge in tandem from their suite of rooms. Its Latin school song still rings around my head - ludus est nobis bonus o sodales... It was sung at every annual speech day in the City Hall by the massed choir of school children, behind that long, high stage on which the assembled worthies sat. That was the very stage where, at weekends, I would listen to Johnny Kidd and the Pirates, Gerry and the Pacemakers and the Beatles.

Firth Park Grammar School was an old-fashioned, disciplinarian sort of a place, and it was sited at the top of Barnsley Road, after a long and leg-wearying bicycle climb up the hill from Fir Vale. The playing fields were on a wind-raked hillside, directly opposite the school, just above Longley Park, where Uncle Kenneth would take me for football practice every Sunday morning. That was the most unfair soccer pitch down which I have ever booted a ball, sloping downhill at a ferocious, off-kilter angle so that during the half that you were obliged to kick uphill, the opposition would pile in at least six goals - and your side would do the same, probably aided by a good, ball-lifting wind - in the second half. Tit for tat then.

Did I distinguish myself at that school? Not especially, not at first. My sciences were always poor, my hold on mathematics tenuous. Like so many other school boys, I usually found myself in a settled mood of sullen distraction as I walked its endless corridors, always looking for the correct subject room, almost always, to my dismay, finding it. Many of the teachers, sweeping by, hands clasped behind backs in their ankle-length black gowns, and without casting so much as a look in our direction, were idle and ferocious, dictating reams of old notes at high speed from ancient green exercise books spread open in front of them. They loved calling us to order at Assembly Hour - 8.30 on the dot - in the school hall.

Mr Taylor, Head of Geography, face set in stone, would be standing on the platform beside the Headmaster and other senior masters, and at a certain moment he would stride forward, position himself behind a wooden lectern, which he would adjust by an inch or so with his foot, and then say 'Right!' - nothing but that - in a voice that chilled the blood. The hubbub and the shuffling of feet by the seven hundred, assembled in their sweaty greasy, refractory rows on the floor of the hall, would stop instantly. This tyrannical Taylor, the least personable of all our teachers, was in the habit, at every geography lesson, of dictating back at us the very notes that he had once had dictated at him, I later came to reflect. This was not teaching at all. It was idleness sustained by his own ferocious, bullying presence. Did I fight back in any way? No, I kept my head down, and took down the dictation that was coming at us at such a bewildering speed just as fast as my left hand would allow. There were also a handful of good things about that school. Our club-footed physics master owned a set of old records of blues recordings, and we would listen to these scratchy masterpieces - the rarest of ten-inch records, acquired from goodness knows where, that he would hold between thumb and finger, so carelessly, at dinner time before slapping them down on to the turntable on his desk in front of a blackboard full of half-erased physics formulae - with rapt attention. The voices of those blind, old black men, badly recorded on street corners in the American South, which I heard at dinner time in that physics lab housed in a prefabricated outbuilding in the playground, became some of the most precious things in the world to me. It was as if a magic circle was being drawn around myself as I listened. And as I name these long dead again now, nearly fifty years later, I feel a slight, complicitous thrill of rediscovery: Blind Lemon Jefferson, Blind Willie Johnson, Bukka Reed. Why did they speak to me in this way, these men who were playing on their beaten up guitars on some street corner, exchanging their precious, home-schooled gifts for the few pence that would enable them to survive for a little while longer? I simply could not fathom the mystery of their appeal, which felt so sudden and so urgent.

They were singing songs of lamentation, those old men, and that strange wailing delivery took my breath away, and moved me then as no massively busted and buttocked opera singer has ever moved me - I still feel an intense antipathy towards the Western European operatic tradition; I feel - I have always felt - that I will never belong to that aristocratic family of musical poseurs, no matter how hard I try. These poor old men on their street corners, playing for a dime or two, wearing the very clothes in which they had slept, they were wholly, marvellously other, and as I listened to them, I raised them up like some public monument. It was as if they were speaking directly to my heart. The songs that they sang, so uncomplicated, and so crudely wrought, struck me as marvels: *take me baby, try me one more time, take me baby, try me one more time. If I do not suit you, keep me a great long time...* It was so simple, and it cut through to the heart of the matter immediately. They were utterly remote from me, their skin colour was different from mine, yet they still, by some miracle, seemed to be at one with everything that I was becoming in my back bedroom in that fairly poor district of north-east Sheffield. How could this be, that they felt so sweat-soaringly near, and yet so far from me? They sang about love, lust, poverty, deprivation, and their tunes were of the utmost simplicity. Which meant that they were within exciting reach of my own meagre, burgeoning abilities as a singer, a guitarist, a songwriter and a poet. They taught me the power of a simple refrain - the repeated phrase - long before I fell in love with the great, culturally high-toned poetry of W.B. Yeats. Within time it became apparent to me that there is a relatively narrow band of themes that never fails to tug at the human heart, and, equally important, that so called serious music spends so much of its time shamelessly stealing from the heart-stopping simplicities of folk song.

So I listened, over and over, to the way a blues man sang his lines, and to the narrow range of chords that he used to such devastating and wonderful effect. I also discovered that the most banal turn of phrase, versifying of the crudest kind, can be raised to great heights by the persuasive powers of the human voice. Even poorly made songs could make you cry. Had it do with the fact that I too was poor, and that this city in which I grew up was a poor place of working people? That sounds like a seductively simple, sociologically pleasing interpretation, and perhaps even a way of transforming this spasmodic account of my upbringing into something a touch heroic.

And then there was that overwhelming moment in a music lesson one idling afternoon, sitting on a tiered bench sufficiently far away to avoid close inspection - so much of school consisted of long and idling afternoons shuffling from ham to ham on old, well used wooden seats; afternoons were so much more slow-moving than mornings - when old and tetchy Mr Parry, the aptly named Welsh head of music, put on a recording of the Nimrod Suite by Elgar, and listening - intently for a change because I had been caught unawares - to the slow build of massed strings towards the piece's devastating, heart-stopping, triumphal conclusion, I was transported by classical music as never before.

It was not until near the end of my school life that everything seemed to change, that I found a reason to work, that work stopped being something imposed upon me like sacks of grain half-slipping from the back of a mule. Poetry seized hold of me. I had no anticipation that such a thing would happen. It came from nowhere. I knew that in part it had something to do with a visceral excitement about private reading that had been encouraged by my passion for Christianity. When I was a Christian, I would read constantly and avidly, but not for its own sake. I was seeking out the truth. At bedtimes I would sit up in bed with my Bible and my little book of daily Bible notes, reading and, pondering, eight to ten lines at a time, and then studying the Bible notes. The Bible itself began to enthral me, its language, its metaphors. It still enthrals me. It digs down deeper than any other book. It seems to pinion our language, and especially the King James Bible, which was translated at the end of the first decade of the seventeenth century. I began to be excited by links between then and now, to recognise how language had evolved, and also how it had stayed the same, how the very same words and phrases had held out the same promises of hope and despair over centuries. I was becoming a part of something wider and larger than myself, so much broader and longer than the street where I had been born or the people amongst whom I had grown up, and it had nothing whatsoever to do with the promises of a personal god. All this dawned on me over the years.

Dylan and the Beatles at the City Hall

There is always so much to be written about Bob Dylan. And yet too many people have written it already. Biographers. Journalists. Hagiographers. That is part of the problem of saying anything whatsoever about the influence of Bob Dylan upon my life as a boy growing up in Sheffield in the 1960s. No matter where we happen to live, he is always too much with us. Too much is known about every step that he has taken. One's memories are subsumed into and, almost overwhelmed by, a giant collective memory, which has been assembled, bit by bit, day by day, by an enormous crowd of adoring witnesses across the globe.

It was not Dylan alone, of course, who caused that decade of the 1960s, the decade of my teenage years, to witness the greatest outpouring of popular music that the world had ever experienced. And the wonder of it all was that many of the inventors and the performers of that music paid a visit to our local concert hall, the Sheffield City Hall in Barker's Pool. The City Hall is not a natural venue for popular music, I recognise that now. It looks, sounds and feels staid and restrained. Its neo-classical façade seems to promises seriousness, edging into dullness. Its acoustics were more suited to the Hallé Orchestra and the natural flamboyance of Sir John Barbirolli, whose wheeling arms and unruly hair I observed with some fascination from the balcony of the City Hall during one or another of those dreary cultural occasions planned by Firth Park Grammar School for the necessary cultural betterment of its sullen boys. We would sit in dutiful rows in our maroon blazers, half-listening.

Yes, the City Hall, for all the limitations of its acoustics, seemed to offer marvels in those days. They came from everywhere, from the American South to Merseyside. The very fact that sound systems were so rudimentary then meant that performers could not get away with trickery of any kind. You saw and heard humankind in the raw, alone in front of a microphone with nothing but a guitar. Roy Orbison was amongst the most intriguing. I had never seen a performer so undemonstrative. He barely moved as he sang. His eyes were concealed behind a huge pair of black glasses which seemed to engulf the greater part of his face. Was he blind perhaps? Probably not. No one had led him onto the stage. Everything was black about him - from the tremendous black quiff down - except for his white, roll-necked sweater. He strummed his black, full-bellied guitar mechanically, without much discernible emotion. He barely moved as he sang. Even his lips seemed barely to open. Everything was contained within the enormous reach and power of his voice, which, having slipped out of his mouth somehow or other, soared to a scarcely credible pitch when he hit the top notes. It was then that you could see, by the trembling of his throat muscles, that he was giving his performance everything that he had to offer. He was not, after all, an inanimate waxwork of himself. And when he had finished, he walked off the stage without so much as a word. He had done all that he needed to do.

Next on stage in the mind's eye come the Beatles, fresh-faced, enthusiastic, driven by the rawness of Lennon's vocals who stood on the right of the stage, almost directly in front of me. He was a little chubby in those days, and tightly contained - like all the rest of them - within what looked shiny maroony-purple terylene suits with collarless jackets. As he played his rhythm guitar, Lennon's knees would flex mechanically, and up and down he would go, up and down, like a doll being jogged about on someone's knee. McCartney looked the most memorable and handsome of the four, holding his left-handed, violin-shaped bass guitar up at an extraordinary angle as he played - just like Bo Diddley, I noticed later. This was the Beatles in the year before 'She Loves You,' before they had begun to write their great songs. They were not exceptional, I thought to myself. They were a part of a new phenomenon called The Mersey Sound. They were no better and no worse than Gerry and the Pacemakers, Billy J. Kramer and the Dakotas, Brian Poole and the Tremeloes and others, I quickly concluded. Had I tipped anyone for the top just then, I would probably have chosen the force and the clarity of the voice of Gerry Marsden, lead singer of Gerry and the Pacemakers, another Liverpool group, over any one of the Beatles.

They all seemed to be in it together, all these young bands, and none more so than the spectacularly colourful Johnny Kidd of Johnny Kidd and the Pirates, with his billowing white piratical shirt, eye patch, cutlass, and shiny black trews. I remember nothing about the songs that he sang or the quality of his voice, and everything about his dazzlingly swashbuckling stage presence. Who needs music when you can swing a blade on stage?

I went to see the Beatles again, and then yet again for the very last time, when they had just released 'She Loves You'. By now their fame had grown and grown, and they were performing on their own. This time, such was the demand for seats, I had to sit in the balcony, and watch them writhing about the stage from a distance. Everything had changed. They were now almost completely inaudible through no fault of their own. Silly girls were throwing themselves around in front of me, clasping their hands to their ears, and screaming uncontrollably. I couldn't have heard the music even if I had wanted to. I stayed to the end of the concert, and then quickly left, in disgust. The rest is too well documented. For all my sniffiness on that night, huge changes had taken place. Elvis the King had been deposed, and my sister's favourite, the crooner Ronnie Hilton, sounded like a laughably tame anachronism. The sixties revolution in popular music was well underway. The popular music of England was beginning to take America by storm.

America fought back. It had its overwhelming surprises too. Bob Dylan strode on to the stage of the Sheffield City Hall on one evening in 1965. I was sitting close to the front of the stalls, on the right hand side, next to my old friend from Ravenfield, Norman West. We were two budding, local singer/songwriters cleaving together, staring in awe at Dylan's left profile as he seemed to prey upon the microphone, inclining his head as he leant into it, snarling and snapping out his every audible word. And it was the words that we – in common with all the rest of this reverentially hushed audience - had come there to listen out for. Never had there been a popular songwriter with such a dazzling talent for words. He was such a small, slight tube of a man, a tiny, fly-like, tousle-headed wisp of a human being, and yet he seemed like a giant that night, hulking inside his black leather jacket, whose sleeves looked just a tad too short for him. He seemed to be holding the plectrum quite finically, hitting the strings hard and brusquely, so that the sound came out urgent and raspingly metallic.

This was pre-electric Dylan at his greatest, singing some of his greatest songs, all freshly minted, and performed for our delectation for the very first time. It was the first time that we had heard 'Baby Blue' or 'Mr Tambourine Man'. The following year, electrified up to the hilt, he would visit Sheffield again. Norman went to that concert too, but I boycotted the event in protest at Dylan's evident betrayal of himself and everything that folk music represented. I was so much older then. I'm younger than that now.

I bought his records, one by one, from Wilson Peck - the racks of LPs were on the far side of the display of grand pianos - or from the basement of Philip Cann down Chapel Walk. It was always a fairly solemn occasion, buying records from Philip Cann. There was an unusual air of respectability about the place. You could always hear music in the air when you idled around the basement, fingering your way through the album sleeves, but it was never pop or - god forbid - rock music. It was always some delicately refined classical number wafting through the air. Consequently, everyone spoke in a hush. It was as if you were in the reading room at the local library. To sample the world of pop music, the newest of the new, you were obliged to go up to the desk, and politely ask to listen to the record of your choice in one of the closed cubicles.

The music, slightly tinny sounding, used to seep out through a speaker lodged somewhere in a corner close to ceiling height. I remember many a time inclining my head up in that direction, as I listened to 'With the Beatles' for the very first time in 1963 or to Joan Baez or Ramblin' Jack Elliott…

Keeping up with the best of what was going on in the world of pop music was a time-consuming business. It meant buying *Disc* and *New Musical Express* every week, cutting out the weekly chart listings, and pasting them into a scrap book. It also meant listening to Alan Freeman - greetings, pop pickers everywhere! - playing that week's top singles on the radio at four o'clock every Sunday afternoon, and being careful to record the programme on my Grundig reel-to-reel tape recorder for careful analysis later.

But it was Dylan who stole all our hearts – and our young minds too. That was the greater part of it, that he was writing extraordinary lyrics that you listened to once, utterly mesmerized by his play of metaphor, his tireless inventiveness - as Norm and I were on that night in 1965 at the City Hall - and then went over and over in your head, puzzling out the meaning. Sometimes it would take me years to understand a particular turn of phrase, and then, all of a sudden, the penny would drop.

The one I have already quoted was such an example of his mysteriousness: *Oh, I was so much older then, I'm younger than that now.* What ever could he mean by that? These words were qualitatively different from anything else that we were listening to. Beside Dylan, the Beatles were nothing as lyricists, although John Lennon did eventually write a handful of songs with words that deserved some attention. And listening to Dylan made you want to be like him, a roaming, footloose guitarist, a hobo, happily adrift without a dollar to his name, out on the wild and windy streets of Sheffield, and a headlong, impulsive song writer into the bargain. I even wrote a song about such a person, and I performed it in front of the prefects and teachers at school. I also tried to perfect the art of sounding like Dylan, all nasally menace, which meant doing my best to sound like the man who had done his best to sound like Woody Guthrie. Who had Woody tried to sound like? I never asked myself that question. I was too busy playing my twelve-string guitar upside down.

Sitting down on my doorstep broke,
Without a penny, without a hope,
Hoping a fairy will bring a smoke,
I'm a down-and-out, a god-forsaken loafer.

In the night, the city streams with light,
Piccadilly glares at awesome height,
But it only gives me a fright,
I'm a down and out, a god-forsaken loafer.

There are times when a tingling runs through me,
But it's forgotten when the night comes.
And I think that I might be someone, maybe.
But I know it's just a dreamland.

So I lie here on my bed all day.
They never want the rent. I never pay.
The sky outside is a dish-cloth grey.
I'm a down-and-out, a god-forsaken loafer.
I'm a down-and-out, a god-forsaken loafer,
I'm a down-and-out, a god-forsaken loafer.

I couldn't exactly be that though, could I, because I was also, in those years of Dylan rapture, a committed Christian who on weekdays wore a maroon school blazer with a large, enamelled Scripture Union badge attached to the lapel. The mysteries of Dylan were obliged to join hands with the mysteries of Christianity. They didn't seem to be at odds with each other. On the contrary, I would play my version of 'God on our Side' to children in the Sunday School class that I was teaching at Trinity Fir Vale Methodist Church. I would write Christian songs in the spirit of Dylan and play them in church. Here are the lyrics of 'His Name', one of those songs, earnest, dirge-like, with its orthodox, slightly damp-squibby conclusion, and written, quite unashamedly, cod rhymes and half-rhymes and all, at the feet of my young master. Yes, Bob Dylan was just eight years older than me. I realized that many, many years later. Which meant that I would never be as old as him, no matter how hard I slashed at the steel strings.

His name was so long that it took me five years to forget it.
He had a book which he gave me that watched me
until I misplaced it.
He had a hand so large that it needed six men to hold it.
He had a will so strong that only he could break it.

Oh, how we sang when he died
And were left to give of ourselves again.

Amidst the flames of that dark room, the tension
was building and building.

Each one looked at the other and wondered
and muttered and willed it.

They were broken apart like crumbs from a loaf that's forgotten.
Yet he haunted them still and was never, no never, forgotten.

Oh, how we sang when he died
And were left to give of ourselves again.

They spoke of his face, of his eyes, of his touch, of his manner.
The innocent ran to him openly. He was a ladder
Up which everyone climbs and, fearfully, seeks his forgiveness.
And he offers it freely to all those who know they are guilty.

Oh, how we sang when he died,
And were left to give of ourselves again.

And alongside Dylan there was the influence of all those old blues
men, many of whom I would never see on stage because they were long
dead. I am talking about Sleepy John Estes, Blind Lemon Jefferson, Big Bill
Broonzy and others. Their records were often quite difficult to come by, but
I found them all the same, at Violet May's record shop in Matilda Street and
other, even more unlikely, places. I found Leadbelly's *Last Sessions* and rare

EPs by Sleepy John Estes and his harmonica-playing cousin at a furniture shop in Rotherham. Violet's shop was the louchest place I had ever visited. Small, untidy, and reeking of Violet's fuggy cigarette smoke, it oozed the sleazy danger of raw jazz. Philip Cann would have died of fear and shame in that place. Christianity. Poetry. Popular music. They were all part of life's great adventure of growing.

Politics

There was a curious mixture of some politics – just a smattering - and no politics at all at 45 Coningsby Road. There was no sustained political debate of any kind, merely a general grumble about the unfairness of life. As a young teenager, I absorbed the left-leaning opinions of Uncle Ken's *Observer*, week in, week out. Hatred of the Germans smouldered on into the 1950s and after, although no one I knew had ever seen one or met one (excepting my grandfather, decades before, at the Somme). Mr Atkin, the jeweller and watch mender down Owler Lane whose large teeth and thick tongue always seemed to get in the way of his speech, also sold a few long-playing records that he kept out of reach behind the counter, and one day he played me an excerpt from a boxed set of Churchill's speeches. For all the heady rhetoric of the words, I found Churchill's manner of speaking strangely sleep-inducing. The voice itself seemed to be speaking from a remote and unreachable past. And what of the world out in the street? Anti-Semitic remarks were still commonly bandied about, although we had no Jewish enemies (or friends) that we could have named. One day, on the upper floor of Boots the Chemists in the centre of Sheffield, I came across a book about Buchenwald. I remember standing there, beside the cosmetics counter, reading it in horror. And what of other racial groups? Everyone seemed to agree that Sheffield's West Indian bus conductors, drafted in to fill a gap, were doing a good job. My mother railed against Pakistan and its peoples, but Jan, one of her closest friends, and our next door neighbour in later years, came from that country, and seemed to possess as many human virtues as anyone else that she knew. Meanwhile, we were rock-solid Labour people. Always had been, always would be. Knew nothing else. Red for Labour and Sheffield United, my football team, blue for the Tories and Sheffield Wednesday, the despised opposition, which always seemed to be better supported and more successful. The constituency was Brightside – a glorious misnomer – and today it is still solid Labour. David Blunkett, our former home secretary, is its MP. And yet there was no discussion of Labour politics in any detail. All we knew was that the Tories - we didn't know any Tories either - were an alien species, remote toffs who were principally dedicated to parting us from the little money that we were fortunate enough to have. My mother would snarl her disgust at them if they appeared on television. There were Tory MPs in Sheffield, but their seats were confined to the outer boroughs, places of unreachable and enviable prosperity.

And yet we never knew ourselves as members of the working class. No such phrase ever passed our lips. Working people, yes, but certainly not a definable class. People were who they were along Coningsby Road, cussed individuals, some to be welcomed, many to be repulsed or, at best, ignored, nose to the ground, when you passed them by. There were sorts who were as good as gold, bad 'uns, and plenty of undefinable, nondescript in-betweens who never seemed to be in or out of any kind of trouble. There was no Communist rhetoric of any kind attached to our tenuous, tribal allegiance to the Labour Party. And yet Communism did come to the door from time to time. There was a Communist bookshop at the Wicker Arches which I used to visit as a teenager - Russian was one of the language options available to us at Firth Park Grammar School during the 1960s. I took Russian at 'O' level and then, my interest quickening, at 'A ' level. It was taught by a clever man we nicknamed Boris - he had written the text book we were using. 'Boris' Hayward had a rolling, shambolic walk, lived with a half-smile forever playing about his lips as if he knew something that you didn't, always wore the same saggy-pocketed, brown tweed jacket, and had large hands which were forever smothered in chalk dust.

Language teaching was different in those years. It was not about the need or the desirability of communicating with other human beings. All we knew were each other, day after blinking day. What is more, we were completely unacquainted with Russia itself. How could we not be? It was so remote from us geographically, and, if anything, it represented a threat - I was learning Russian at the height of the Cold War. Missiles were poised to strike. What is more, there was so little emphasis upon Russian as a spoken language in those years. It counted for so little in the exams, so why bother about talking? Reading was much more interesting.

This sense of our remoteness is so understandable in those years before even Freddie Laker had taken his first giant step in the direction of international air travel. Yes, these were the years before travel revolutionised our ability to move about the world, and to be in the midst of strange peoples uttering strange tongues within a matter of hours. Even to go to London was to travel quite magically far in those days. One of my most prized toys from Redgates on the Moor, that toyshop we could have lived in forever had accommodation been available, was a brown bakelite slide projector which came complete with a disc of images. The most prized showed the sights of London: Big Ben, Westminster Abbey, the Houses of Parliament. London was as far as our ideas of the exotic extended, and I did not even travel that far until I was about fourteen years old. It is therefore unsurprising that we never heard Russian spoken by a Russian - well, we would occasionally hear the beginnings of a remark by a small, snarling, bear-like man called Kruschev on the television - at the time of the Cuban

Missile Crisis, for example - but the Russian that he was speaking, then as now, would soon disappear beneath the words of the English translator. We never met a Russian either. What I principally knew of Russia, its customs and its peoples, was gleaned from reading extracts from the great Russian classics of an earlier era, and these could be bought at very little cost in their subsidised, Soviet-era editions at the Communist bookshop near the Wicker Arches. It was much the same with other countries, too. When I went to a *lycée* in Paris at the age of 16, I discovered that the French children were not only studying Charles Dickens, but that they believed the London of Charles Dickens to be essentially the London of today, complete with its pea-souper fogs. We were all equally ignorant of, and superior to, each other. And, if my mother had had her way, we would have continued to be. There was nowhere quite so dangerous as Elsewhere.

That is not quite all that there is to be said about our comfortable politics of insularity. One day I met a young Communist who was as alive as you or me. What is more, he wasn't much older than me. I ran into him one day, quite by chance, in the Communist bookshop. Some days later he came to Coningsby Road to talk to me about the coming revolution, and of how I could play my part in helping to expose the pernicious habits of top-hatted capitalists. I had read the *Communist Manifesto* by then, but to me it was just another example of godlessness. I listened intently to what he said as he stood on the back doorstep. He was so vehement, so assured, just as confident of his own opinions as I had been when I tried to convince others of the need to invite Jesus into their lives. Were we more similar to each other than we would ever have dared to admit? What I remember most of all about that visit was the brown, ankle-length greatcoat that he was wearing, and how magnificent it looked on him. I later saw such greatcoats in Soviet-era paintings. Three years later I was at university. One of the first things I did was to buy an ankle-length greatcoat, uncannily similar to his, from an army surplus store. I let it weigh heavily on my shoulders with enormous pride. By then I was striding out as a proud, left-wing atheist.

Whitsuntide

It's a fine and vivid early morning in Coningsby Road. I wake up in my small attic bed, tucked in beside the wall. There's a pale light seeping down through the skylight, waking things up, letting me see yesterday's clothes in a heap on the chair, waiting to be put on. I know immediately that there's something to remember, though I'm not quite sure what, not straightaway. My body does though because I'm kicking my legs out in excitement like a mad eye, pumping them one after the other like the pistons of my best Christmas steam engine, with its gleaming brass boiler that gets so red hot to the touch just before those pistons start turning, and the steam comes pothering out of the tall tunnel like dangerous magic. Yes, it's already getting light, and things are happening downstairs. I know that because I catch the kettle's dying whistle in the kitchen downstairs. Someone's mashing. Papa's mashing tea in the teapot! When I look to the left, I see that there's only one body in the bed next to mine, and it's not very near, but quite far away. That hump, thrashing about a bit, is my big sister, Pat. Mum and papa must be downstairs then, messing about in the kitchen, getting ready for...what though?

Then I suddenly remember. It's Whitsuntide today! It's Whitsunday! I love Whitsunday. There are only three really special days in the year, and Whitsunday is one of them. There's Christmas - number one by a mile - when you go down to the kitchen, and see presents in two pillow cases laid side by side on the kitchen table, Pat's next to mine, two white, bulging sacks full of funny and exciting shapes. You never know what they are. You start off by feeling them, with mum looking on, beaming. Then there's Guy Fawkes Night... No, it's definitely not one of those usual boring Sundays when nothing ever happens, and none of the shops are ever open, not even Gabbitas' for the gobstoppers that plop out of the machine outside in the street - straight down the little chute at the front - if you stick a penny in, and such like. I race down the attic stairs and bump down the second flight of twelve steep steps to the kitchen on my behind. It doesn't really hurt though. Mum's just standing there with her arms folded at the bottom, but she's smiling as well.

It's a bit of a bother getting ready for going out at Whitsuntide - there are so many smart clothes to put on - but it's worth it in the end. There's that many folks on the Bottom when you get there, Pat and me, mum, Uncle Ken, papa and nanny. Everybody's got their best things on.

Even Mrs Lockin's all dolled up and taken her curlers out. Nanny's wearing the straw hat she wears on the Blackpool promenade, when they sit facing the sea, with papa leaning on his stick and just looking. Pat's got a pretty flowery dress on that she twizzles round in to show just how far out it goes. I want her to give me a swizz like she usually does in the back yard, grabbing me up by the armpits, and then swinging me round and round and round so that when she drops me, I can't even walk straight. I'm like a drunk man when that happens, and everybody laughs at me through the kitchen window. She can't do that though because there's too many people crowded on the pavement opposite Banners, waiting for the big parade to begin. Everybody's down there today like they always are on Whitsunday, all dressed up in their new clothes because it's such a special day. Then suddenly I hear it starting from far away, up in Firth Park direction, and I start pummeling on Uncle Ken's legs to make him pick me up so that I can see what's happening, and now I'm on his shoulder and he says to me: the weight of two elephants lies on this head of mine, like he always does to make me laugh, and I always laugh because it's always funny, the way he says it.

And then it's happening, here they all are, all the Sunday School children from the local area, marching past in their best Sunday clothes, and they've all got their banners at the front saying Ellesmere Road Sunday School and such like, and these great big banners are being held up on poles by big, serious-looking children with sashes across their suits and their dresses. And in front of these waving, swaying banners, the bands are marching ahead, with buglers and cornet players and trumpeters and the big drum booming loud enough to make your ears shudder. And out in front of the parade the man with a mace comes, twirling and spinning it in his fingers, and not once dropping it, no matter how many times he spins it, and once he even throws it up in the air and catches it again. And I wish I was that man with the mace, just once, but I couldn't be, could I, because I don't even go to Sunday School, not yet.

When it's all passed by, all those smart, marching children with their banners, and all the bands booming and rasping along, we all come on behind, wave upon wave of us, loads of people marching up the centre of the road along the tram tracks towards Firth Park itself where everyone will be gathering, thousands of us, having a great big picnic of egg and cress sandwiches and bottles of bright red Tizer and white fizzy lemonade - Tizer and lemonade together for once, not one or the other - because it's Whitsuntide, and not some usual Saturday dinner time with Workers Playtime blaring out of the radio, and papa flashing his carving knife and

115

steel before he starts to carve it all up, the Saturday joint of beef that's turned into rissoles from the mincer by Monday, rissoles mixed up with bits of stale weekend bread crumbled into crumbs, not half so good...

Potatoes are always good though. Potatoes never let you down. Yorkshire pudding neither.

Nature

I have spoken of nature as being conspicuous by its absence in Fir Vale. The longer I go on writing this memoir, the deeper I see into the situation, and the more I come to appreciate that what I wrote a few days ago is not quite true. There was nature in and around Fir Vale, but it was only there in fits and starts, half-forgotten remnants, hiding behind hoardings, or just a little further away than you were usually inclined to go. You had to look for it. Having said that though, the first place I might have looked was just behind our rockery, over the wall from the backyard. A piece of scrubby ground was there, full of tenacious weeds, thistles and other hardy, unkillable devils. Not much else. No one cultivated this patch of ground. No one seemed to own it. It never looked as if it wanted to be owned or claimed. It looked as if it might have repulsed anyone who even had the temerity to try. I was a little bit frightened of this plot of land. Its curious emptiness worried me, and the aggressive, indomitable quality of its weeds. Its atmosphere seemed to be pushing up against the wall behind our rockery. I always feared that something harmful might begin there. Nothing ever did. You could see beyond that scrubby plot to the backs of the houses on Fir Vale Road, and in fact across to the back steps of the very house where Blondie lived. Yes, that was the name she went by, the woman who lived in that house. It was my mother's name for her, so it is the name that I shall give her. Blondie was tough and quite fierce looking, fast-walking too, as if she always had somewhere to go as quickly as possible, and she always wore curlers underneath her head scarf. She looked as if she belonged to that neglected plot of ground, and as if she might even be related to it in some way.

That piece of land was separated from our rockery by a wall topped by a wire-mesh fence. One day a bit of that wall fell down - goodness knows why. Not entirely, but in part, and a man came to mend it. He was a very slow and meticulous worker, this man, and he always came dressed in his blue overalls and clutching a trowel. And then he would set to work, lifting up each brick separately, and then setting it down with great meticulousness. I would watch him work. I would even climb up on the rockery to get a better look, but he would never speak to me. When I asked my mother why he didn't talk, she told me that he was a Pole, and that he was mute. Which meant that even if he had wanted to speak to me, it would have been impossible.

Years after this man left, never to return, I still thought in my heart of hearts that all Poles were mutes. In later life I even wrote a story called 'The Silentiary'. It was about a woman who could not speak. She was the daughter of a Polish aristocrat.

Ten minutes walk up Herries Road, and you came to Roe Woods. The entrance to those woods on the end of Norfolk Road is practically opposite the side gate to the Northern General Hospital. Even when I was a boy, the atmosphere of Roe Woods was sinister, strangely set apart. It always felt a bit like a dangerous thrill to play there. It was not an easy wood to negotiate. A steep climb up the main path took you to a levelling plain of scrubby grass. As you made that walk uphill, the ground fell away, quite dramatically, to your right into a ravine through which a small stream would riddle its uncertain way. I last visited those woods during the month before my mother's death in the autumn of 2009. As with Wincobank Hill just a couple of miles away, it had changed dramatically. The dwarf oaks had matured into towering trees. That stream was choked with beer cans and other assorted rubbish. I felt much more enclosed by the wood than ever before. The wood itself felt neglected, untended, unloved. The allotments at the top end of the wood had disappeared to make way for a new housing estate. Which means that the seven ponds in which I had once fished for minnows had gone. No one was with me on that day, and yet I felt spied, even preyed, upon. This poem summarises the atmosphere of the hours that I spent there.

Roe Woods

It is likely to be here once again that I find you.
This is the spot where you would always be sitting,
Shoeless, arm carelessly thrown back, peering idly
into that clump of bushes.
We shared the pleasures of this drifting woodland.

It is likely to be tomorrow that I shall chance upon you.
You were always waiting for me tomorrow, then tomorrow,
ever ready to give me your signal.
It was always a smile that you gave me, barely noticeable,
And yet I saw it, at no matter what a distance
I might happen to be standing.

It is always here that I shall remember you.
It is raining today, adding some weight to my shoulders.
I lick at the drops with my tongue's tip, I smile,
and I idle.
I am, as ever, expectant for you. There is no one here
to prevent you.

But there were many other places too that might be called nature in
the raw, even when they seemed to be there by default. There was the
cinder track behind the advertising hoardings on Barnsley Road, just at the
back of the Sunbeam cinema, where we would have our cycle races and,
just down the hill from there, the untamed spot behind the Cannon Hall,
an old public house, that fell into ruins during my childhood and whose
lonely, dangerous, half derelict rooms we used to explore, and, just behind
Skinnerthorpe Road nearby, the allotments where Uncle Ken and papa and
I used to grow our potatoes and rhubarb and spring onions and lettuces.
   It was on the cinder track in front of our allotment gate that one of the
most frightening episodes of my childhood took place. I was coming out
of that gate one day - I must have been eleven or twelve years old - when
a boy on a bike came tearing towards me. I recognised him. He lived in a
street nearby called Barretta Street. He asked me what I was doing there. He
told me never to go there again or something terrible would happen to me.
I had never known such fear as I felt on that day. He was perhaps three or

four years older than me. His hair was long and matted. I stood, speechless, not knowing how to respond. He didn't hit me. Instead, he thrust out his finger and made a kind of screwing gesture in the air. Then, all of a sudden, he wheeled round with his bike, spraying cinders into my face, and cycled back up the track. I told no one about it. I somehow persuaded myself that it would be cowardly to tell anyone. I saw him just once after that, and I was not alone on that second occasion, but for several years after, I lived in fear that he would come after me. Whenever I walked past the end of his street, I would cast a nervous, side-long glance in its direction. Yes, I knew exactly where he lived.

Food

Way, I never bothered about food that much, except for sweets from Gabbitas' on t' Bottom and sweet stuff. Chewin gum were best, Wrigleys an' Beach Nut. Papa had his own special stuff like oxtail and chitterlings and chines an' tongue. He were only one who liked that sort of stuff - he kept it on t' top shelf in t' pantry - so he cooked it for himself. I loved trifle at Christmas, that great big bowl of it, and dripping sandwiches for tea with loads of brown gravy oozing out, an' kippers oppened out wi' slices of bread spread wi' Stork marg so you didn't even notice fish bones cos they were so small any road. Tinned strawberries wi' carnation milk were great and mandarin oranges an' all.

For special tea mum'd oppen a tin of red salmon an' we'd all get a little bit of it next to a few leaves of lettuce, an' a skinny lookin spring onion. Lettuce were rubbish. It never tasted of owt at all, even when you shook loads of vinegar on it. Beef were all right except for gristly bits, but lamb were rubbish. Chicken were too expensive, mum allus said that. We aren't made of money, she'd say, tuttin at me. I hated lamb. I couldn't stand the taste of it in my mouth. Stinkin, slimy greens were horrible an' all, an' hash nanny made wi' all them bits of fatty meat swimming in't greasy gravy. You never knew them fatty bits were there till you got them in your mouth. I allus wanted to spit them out cos they made me feel sick. Sometimes I did or put 'em in an 'anky. Then one Saturday dinner time - Workers Playtime were on't radio, an there were red Tizer and fizzy lemonade on t' kitchen table - Uncle Ken tricked me. He said them little bits he'd just cut up and stuck on my dinner plate were beef. He promised me that they were. I were right suspicious. I believed him though because he were Uncle Ken, weren't he, and Uncle Ken wouldn't lie to me. I poked at them a bit, then I popped one in. Not that bad. Then they all laughed at me, and pointed. It were lamb after all. They'd tricked me. Uncle Ken'd tricked me. Worst things though were blinking rissoles on Monday dinner time. They used to put bits of weekend meat in't mincer an' grind it up until it came out like little brown worms. Nanny used to pat it into little fat circles of meat an' add some gluey egg she'd mixed up in t' brown mixing bowl an' all to mek rissoles. They were rubbish, rissoles. They never tasted of owt at all. I loved a glass of milk before goin' to bed, way it tasted so thick an so creamy when it went down, thick an slow an' all. Not like watter which didn't taste of owt at all, and went rushing down your throat. I hated watter. Mum allus made us gargle wi' it when we had a sore throat, watter an' Saxa salt. Only good thing were noise of garglin in front of t' sink so you didn't spit water all over the show accidentally on purpose, grrrrrrrrrrrrrrrr. It were like revvin' up Morris Minor on cold mornins when it never wanted to start an' Uncle Ken got in a right old state about it. Milk were sticky an' smeary on your lips for ages after you'd drunk it. You could taste it inside your mouth an all. I loved that. Mum allus said: off to bed then, milky lips, an' I'd smile at her, an' she'd smack me one, not hard though cos she were only kiddin, then she'd dash after me wi' a cloth to wipe it off. I'd bang glass down on t' table, an she'd say: don't smash it then. Ooh, you are a little limb, you. Ger away wi yer, yer little devil. You never know when enough's enough, you. You're forever mitherin me.

I didn't either.

Pubs

Pubs were places I loved. My mother never said she minded either. She never said owt about it. It was as if there were a magic circle drawn around my bad habits. I didn't really start going to them till I was about eighteen. I hated the taste of beer until then. It tasted so sour and so nothingy. I learnt to love it though because it were what you drank when you went to pubs, weren't it? You couldn't not do it.

The best was the Mulberry Tavern, down a little alley in the centre of town, behind Saxone's shoe shop. I never went to shoe shops unless I really had to. My sister never went to owt else. She were a big shopper, Pat, allus comin back laughin' an' rollin' her eyes wi' great big bundles o' stuff. Mulberry were great. I'd have three pints or so there, all on my own. Sometimes I'd take a book of poems with me. Poetry books were great for pubs. Poetry and beer were very good companions. The point about poetry is that its meanings come to you quite slowly, drifting in, and even then you're never quite sure you've got it right. You might have. You might not have. It all depends. Next day it might mean something slightly different. The point is to be there with it, letting it work on you, nursing it, like a mouthful of beer. No one else needs to be involved at all. You don't want them involved either. It's none of their business.

Pubs were a bit like poems to me then. You could go in to them, order a pint from nice looking woman at bar, and then just sit there soaking it all up. Nobody looked up when you went in. That's what pubs were for, for folks to drift in to, formlessly, like souse, just because you felt like it. You might just catch her eye. That could be good. Or she might just give you a nasty stare back when she caught you doin' it as she were pullin a pint because she didn't want you to be starin' at her, you cheeky little bugger. There'd probably be hardly anybody there in that pub, just two or three old blokes who were mindin' their own business an' all, starin' at their glasses as if they were thinking about summat. You could look at people when you felt like it, when you weren't looking down at your book, but you didn't have to, and nobody bothered their heads over it if you did or you didn't. You had a right to be there, sitting nice and peaceful in a chair, just watching and drifting. Only slightly difficult bit were leaving when you felt it had come time to leave. That weren't very nice because when you got up to go, and picked up your book, everybody else felt they had a right to look at you then, as if to say: where are you off to now then, you soft little bugger?

What gave you a right to leave just now when we're still sitting here, right as rain, nursing our pints? So that were awkward, leaving, making that quick dash to the door, and then heaving a huge sigh of relief when you'd got out into the drizzly cool of the street. If you'd had a few, you might even walk home, it were fun floating home after a few pints, seein' nobody worth seeing, drifting up streets and down. One day you might even take a door key out of your pocket and scratch a car just for the fun of it.

Away

Early on a cold, late-February day in 1968. Breakfast time at Coningsby Road. The lights are all on in the kitchen, the fire is blazing, and the kettle's on the hob. My mother is fussing over not much at all, and my grandfather is patiently, silently working his way through his bacon and mushrooms. The mushrooms are hard and small and black, ferociously over-cooked, like little bits of shrapnel - he's often talked about shrapnel in his leg in the past, sometimes jokingly, but I don't remember ever having seen it. All I usually saw when he pulled up his trouser leg was the expandable silver band that kept his checked sock up.

There are just the three of us there at Coningsby Road now, down from the busy, noisy six that we were for much of my time there. We are all waiting for something, and we don't know how long we will have to endure the suspense. Weeks before, I had done the entrance exam for Cambridge University in a small, hot room at the top of the turret at Firth Park Grammar School. I had also attended interviews with the unbending Director of English Studies at Queens' College, and the much more genially companionable senior tutor with his welcoming smile and his ancient-looking, mutton-chop whiskers.

It was Stanley, my school teacher, who had recommended Queens' College, Cambridge to me, for the fact that it was known to be an affable place, welcoming of boys from grammar schools. He himself had gone to Oxford. In fact, he had studied under a celebrated scholar of abstruse languages called J.R.R. Tolkien, who was not to enjoy global fame until long after his death. Those interviews at Cambridge had not gone well. Taciturnity and a lack of confidence. An inability to speak out about what I knew I knew. A deep unease in the company of strangers. Some of this burden had been inherited from my mother, I knew that. It had felt, all told, like alien ground, that small market town amidst the flatlands of the Fens, which also happened to boast the most extraordinary spectacle of ancient buildings backing on to a small river that I had ever seen in my life. It had felt like two towns in one to me, that place. I had seen no evidence of heavy industry anywhere, nowhere that grown men might go to in their hundreds and thousands to earn an honest living. There were no such places in Cambridge. In fact, there was one - a Pye factory - but it was kept well away from the sheer pomp of the ancient buildings of Cambridge University.

No, it had not gone well, that visit, no one had offered me a place on the strength of what I had said - well, I had said, truth be known, so mumblingly little - and now everything hinged upon whether or not I had been able to claim lost ground in the written examination. I had prepared for those tests furiously, reading every book on the long book list that my teacher had given me. Every spare moment had been given over to study. I felt utterly engulfed by words of the writers I had read. I was almost living their lives. I was now writing poetry regularly too, pouring it out into notebooks, emphasising my own set-apartness from my family, living a life of my own in my attic bedroom beneath the skylight. In spite of the fact that my mother had no knowledge of or much interest in any part of what I was doing, she gave me enormous, prideful support. She was willing me to succeed at something utterly remote from her own experiences or her own understanding. All she knew, with this extraordinary sense of abstract pride, was that I was moving in a certain direction. Did she ever acknowledge to herself that it would take me, physically, beyond her reach, and that I would never again live with her, that her life companion would disappear forever, removing himself to a life that she would never share or fully comprehend? No. Her pride in what I might achieve absorbed all her attention.

Then, on that late-winter morning, there was a knock at the back door. My mother opened it. One of my teachers, Spike Johnson, was standing there on the back door step, smiling back at her. She let him indoors, quickly closing the door behind him on that perishing morning. It was an embarrassment to me to see one of my school teachers in that house. It was not where they belonged. As ever, Spike's eyeballs looked red-rimmed and filmy and bulbous – as if he might have just plucked them up from a mug of salty water, and popped them back into his eye sockets. He was holding a letter in his hand which gave me the news that we had been waiting for so eagerly. He told me that I had been accepted at Queens' College, Cambridge - yes, it seems that he knew already, that he had opened the letter. What is more, I had won an Exhibition, which was a minor scholarship. This guaranteed me £40 a term in addition to the full grant that I would also be receiving from the government and the local authority. It would cost my family nothing to send me to Cambridge University, and I would discover in due course, and to my astonishment, that I would be richer than in any previous time of my life. How otherwise could I have bought, during my first term in residence, a splendid, top-of-the-range Hacker record player, a boxed set of the Collected Music of Anton Webern and, from Ryder and Amies on King's Parade, a black opera cloak lined with silk the colour of lemons?

Needless to say, my mother was deliriously happy for me. There was no one that she did not tell. She boasted on every corner that her son was finally proven to be a superior being, ut   ʼʸ different from the rest.

And every succeeding year thereafter, she would tell me stories of accosting total strangers in boarding houses by the seaside with news of my almost unimaginable achievements. She was utterly at one with me during my moment of exquisite triumph. And, in common with me, she knew almost nothing whatsoever about this alien, elitist environment set in the drizzly, damp, monotonous flatlands of East Anglia, so utterly different, physically and in spirit, from the reassuring hilliness of the north of England. My Uncle Ken and his wife, the most respectable faces of my family, transported me to my new lodgings in Maids Causeway by car, smoothly and sedately, but that is not the memory that clings to me. That was not the way in which I usually got to Cambridge in the four succeeding years. My usual method was to stand alone beside the motorway slip road at the Tinsley Viaduct, in the shadow of the mighty twin cooling towers, rucksack across my back, holding out a thumb. That, at least, was a reminder and a confirmation of my imagined years as a guitar-strumming hobo on the streets of Sheffield. Sooner or later a filthy van or lorry would screech to a halt, and transport me, at least part of the way, in the direction of the rest of my life.

Lords of the Sportsman

Some time in the late spring of 1968, I'm light-headedly walking down the hill from the Sportsman public house near the top of Barnsley Road, singing an old blues song to myself, courtesy of Sleepy John Estes from Brownsville, Tennessee, underneath my breath: 'If the river was whiskey, lord, and I was a divin' duck,/ If the river was whiskey, lord, and I was a divin' duck, I would dive down to the bottom, never would come up...' This song is in my repertoire that I have been building up over the past couple of years. I've spent the evening drinking four or so pints of John Smith's with my school friends, all sixth-formers at Firth Park Grammar School. I'm so light-heatedly proud of all of us. We are the future, I have little doubt of that. That's what the beer is telling me, and it's a powerfully persuasive message. Let me name them now, all the better to get a purchase on their presence there on that Sunday night: Trevor Stacey, who still lives a few yards down from this pub, and who is the Rimbaud of our group, a quietly cussed literary flaneur-cum-closet-revolutionary, with hair as wild and unruly as you could ever see. This secretive, intellectually precocious boy, who finds it almost impossible to do justice to his own extraordinary mind in an examination room, will nevertheless soon be offered a place at Oxford University. He will take up that place - and then, quite soon after, leave again. Next in line is John Pilley, careful, handsome, clever, temperamentally seemingly docile, who will become a fine carpenter. Tom Webster I leave for last. Tom is the most wayward and unpredictable of us all. Already he is smoking furiously as he talks at us about the significance of black holes and the death of god. He will go up to Warwick University in the autumn of that year, where quite soon he will be living in a tree house, high on the life of the late 1960s. By the spring of 1969, he will be sending me pills of LSD through the post to my Cambridge College address. Alarmed, I will flush them down the college lavatory.

When this precious group disperses, I make my way alone down hill to Fir Vale. Soon I come level with the Sunbeam Fish Bar on the corner of Coningsby Road, my street. The cinema I would once have seen on the other side of the road is no longer there. The wrecker's ball has seen to that. But the fish and chip shop is still there, and I walk in for the umpteenth time in my life. It's hot in there, and warm and bright. The air is full of the noise of spitting fat; leaning heaps of sheets from the local newspaper are on the counter. I stare across at the rows of pieces of battered haddock and cod on their glass shelves, singling one out in my mind's eye as I salivate. Directly beneath this mouth-watering display are the gleaming metal covers of the deep rectangular vats in which they furiously cook the chips. They are thrown back, concertina-like, as usual - my god, how furiously that chip fat spits when the milk-white chips are thrown in by the plastic bowlful, like so many victims sacrificed to the lions! I'm ravenously hungry. I'm always hungry after beer. I order my usual from the cheery, fat-armed woman in the white mob cap: haddock and chips. No, not mushy peas, thanks. I hate those slimy, mushy, eerily green things. What I'm looking forward to is that first taste of a hot - too hot! - chip, caught up on the end of a little wooden, two-fingered stick on the tongue's end, of throwing it round and round the inside of my mouth until it cools down enough to bite down on it, and then chewing it, hard and fast. Ah, chips! The sweet reek of malt vinegar in the nostrils as you walk out of doors, clutching that bag of fish and chips wrapped in yesterday's *Green Un*, and take a bit of both at once, a big bite of battered haddock, the sweetness of haddock caught inside the crispness of the batter, together with a chip or two. The key is to fill your mouth with them, both at once, and, throwing a quick left turn after you've gone down hill for a few paces, make your way along Coningsby Road where a cup of hot, sweet tea will soon be brewing, and your mother, standing at the sink with her back to you in her blue flowery pinny, will be tossing a quick, flighty laugh at you back over her shoulder, not really minding that you're not quite all there because, there or not, you'll always be who you are - just as, for then at least, you'll always be where you are and nowhere else, and nothing can ever really change, can it, you soft bugger?

The Death of Coningsby Road

Coningsby Road died in the early 1980s, long after I had left it to live elsewhere. The wrecker's ball that had destroyed the Sunbeam came to visit. And even then not all of it died. Half of the street on the other side of the road still remains. Goodness why that should have been spared. But our side of the street was not spared. Nothing that my mother did to try to save our house was sufficient in the end. It had to go. It had outlived its usefulness. It was a slum. It belonged to an undesirable past of unacceptable social deprivation. In short, it had to go in order to make way for the brightness and the prosperity of the future. Other roads nearby went before Coningsby Road itself - Blyde Road, for example, at right angles to our street, which ran down to the shops at Fir Vale Bottom. That too had been a single row of late nineteenth-century, red-brick terraced housing. That too had its row of asphalted backyards, one to share amongst several houses, strung across with washing lines, occupied, in the top corner, by the outside privies. Somehow - call it preposterous social snobbery if you like - my mother regarded the houses in Blyde Road as slightly inferior to ours, and when I visited them, I found myself tending to agree with her. There were no huge stains of damp on our bedroom walls. But was this any reason for feeling slightly superior?

I felt little about the demolition of Coningsby Road when it happened. I have felt more in later years. News of it came from my English teacher Stanley in a letter sent to me in London in 1983. Eight years later Stanley himself would be dead. He told me that he had walked past the end of the road just a few days before, and that he had seen that the houses were gone. An old woman had been standing on the corner as he passed by, contemplating the rubble. They'll grass it over, and then they'll let it rot. According to Stanley, that's what this woman had said to him. It had the ring of truth about it, her comment. I had seen it happen so often, houses, entire streets of houses, being swept away in preparation for...nothing at all. If there were plans, the plans were jettisoned or superseded by other plans, or the money ran out. Or the vision. There were always so many provisional visions of the future to be contemplated.

My mother stayed there, almost to the bitter end, with her second husband, Wilfred. Little by little, the wreckers encroached upon her. All the houses in the street were demolished barring the ones that stood, boarded up, to the left and the right of her. She experienced a near heroic siege mentality. Pugnaciously obdurate to the last, she became a thorn in the side of the local council. It was the most public moment of her life, and something of which she remained proud for the remainder of it. The council tried to re-locate her to elsewhere in the city. She drove a hard bargain. She would only leave if they found her a house in the district of Sheffield where she most wanted to live, the district which she remembered having loved as a young woman when she was living at Crimicar Lane. So the council, recognising the need to buy off this plucky nuisance of a woman, offered her a choice of two houses in Totley, on the south-western edge of town, almost abutting the corner of the Peak District National Park. The first house was too contemptibly small, the second, in Green Oak Road, as close to her idea of perfection as she could ever have wished. It even had its own garden, something that she had always wanted.

I would like to tell you that she was happy there, on higher, breezier ground, amongst her new neighbours, on the spirit-lifting fringes of the natural beauty of the Peak District, but that would be to lie. Dorothy was almost never happy in the company of near neighbours, anywhere. Along with the furniture, she had made the fatal mistake of taking herself with her. These new neighbours were as bad as all the rest. They were either too neglectful or too nosey-parkerish. In short, other people could never win. Intermittently, she and Wilf would return to Coningsby Road. Her second marriage, in her sixties, had given her the possibility of happiness - and a new lease of life. She even passed her driving test at the third attempt. She and her second husband would drive down to their old haunts in Fir Vale at the weekend in order to feel that sweetly tormenting mingling of impotent rage and despair that the newly dispossessed so often feel. There was nothing to be done about it of course, nothing at all. Times had changed. Everything that they knew - the familiar faces, the familiar shop windows - was either going or had already disappeared The old community had been broken into pieces and dispersed to the four winds. And my mother, alone, in the vanguard of the spirited combatants, had landed, both feet comfortably on the ground, in leafy Totley amongst the Liberal Democrat voters, and within breathing distance of the detested Tories.

Eventually, our side of Coningsby Road came to life again. New houses were built on our side of the street, quite different in shape from ours. The terraces of yesteryear were gone, to be replaced by the cube-like agglomerations of modernity. All trace of their ground plans had been obliterated.

Do I still care about that house? It had little to commend it. It was one of hundreds of thousands of its kind. Although solidly built - there were no damp stains on the walls, no smells of mildew except at the back of certain cupboards - it was wretchedly small, and utterly undistinguished architecturally. You were no sooner inside by the back door than you were outside again in the street. And yet I cared for it - and I still find myself caring for it. It was the site of my growing, the place where the seeds of my own life began to burgeon. The very fact of its being so small appealed to me because small places feel pleasingly secretive and sequestered. As William Blake once wrote, tiny things have the capacity to be worlds unto themselves. They can expand, grow bigger and yet bigger still, in the mind and the imagination.

And then, it was gone, as if it had never been. It was not even gone in the way Stanley's house had disappeared for me. That house had still remained after his death even though he himself and all his belongings had gone from it. No, my house had vanished irreversibly. Particular details pain me when I think back to that fact. I find myself picking my way back down the cellar steps. They were always so badly illuminated, those steps. The light in the cellar itself, a pale yellow, was always so meagre. That's where I always kept my wooden sledge, which I would drag up the road to Longley Park with Uncle Ken when February snow was on the ground. There was a steep hillside in Longley Park where, at a particular moment in the year, that sledge would come into its own. Before setting out, Uncle Ken and I would grease the runners to make it speed downhill all the faster. No one had remembered to remove that sledge before they locked the back door of Coningsby Road for the very last time. That sledge remained, reared up against the back wall, still waiting for some future winter.

My dear elder sister Pat would not agree with me about the merits of Coningsby Road. She detested the place, its meanness, its slightly insanitary squalor. She could not leave soon enough for bigger and airier realms. I too now inhabit similar realms, but I hold the two possibilities in balance within myself, the fascination of the small, beside the undeniably expansive appeal of the large. We are all one, I believe, but we are also several. There is no removing oneself from what one was - once upon a time. And what one was once will remain, forever. Everything always changes. And everything remains the same.

And finally, I must ask myself, as honestly as possible: what has this family of mine bequeathed to me? My mother has given me her undying love, and a horror of almost all social situations involving more than two people, the first of these being myself. And this horror includes at best a deep-seated unease, and at worst a boundless dread, of finding myself trapped in a chair, any chair will do, for hours at a time, around a dinner table, lit with candles, in the company of relatives or near strangers. Hearing her express so many rash, ridiculous and wrong-headed opinions about the world and its peoples has bequeathed to me a kind of bullying, boorish rashness too, which has served me well when in the employ of newspapers. To my grandfather Harold, I owe a boundless anxiety about falling headlong into pennilessness, of being reduced once again to the status of a gutter-snipe; and also an unstoppably wilful determination to pursue my own endeavours as a writer through the thickest and the thinnest of grey Yorkshire skies. And to my dear Uncle Ken, I owe what I have learnt as a writer, that power to be cloistered, shored up, inside myself, and to incubate there my own laughably extravagant dreams of penmanship.

About the author:

Award-winning writer Michael Glover is a Sheffield-born, London-based poet, art critic, fiction writer, editor and publisher who has contributed regularly to the *Independent, The Times,* the *Financial Times,* the *New Statesman* and *The Economist.* He is also a London correspondent for *ArtNews,* New York. His on-line international poetry journal, *The Bow-Wow Shop* (www.bowwowshop.org.uk) appears three times a year. His new collection of poetry, *Only So Much,* is published by Savage Poets Collective of Sheffield. He was born in Fir Vale, Sheffield, and read English at Queens' College, Cambridge.